THE SELF AND THE OTHER IN THE ONTOLOGIES OF SARTRE AND BUBER

Sylvain Boni

UNIVERSITY
PRESS OF
AMERICA

Copyright © 1982 by **Sylvain Boni**

University Press of America, Inc.

P.O. Box 19101, Washington, D.C. 20036

All rights reserved

Printed in the United States of America

ISBN (Perfect):0-8191-2853-8
ISBN (Cloth):0-8191-2852-X

TABLE OF CONTENTS

ABBREVIATIONS OF WORKS MOST FREQUENTLY CITED v

INTRODUCTION 1

      Footnotes 7

PART ONE

Chapter

I.   HISTORICAL BACKGROUND OF THE CONCEPT
     OF THE OTHER 8

     Footnotes 30

PART TWO

II. THE OTHER IN THE ONTOLOGY OF SARTRE 35

     In-Itself and For-Itself
     The Existence of the Other
     Sartre's Concept of the Other
     The Look
     Shame
     The Body
     Facticity
     The Body for Others
     The Third Ontological Dimension of
       the Body
     Concrete Relations with the Other
     Being-With (Mitsein) and the "We"

     Footnotes 82

III. OBSERVATIONS ON SARTRE'S POINT OF VIEW . . . 87

     Ontology
       Ethics
       Community

     Footnotes 106

PART THREE

IV. THE OTHER IN THE ONTOLOGY OF BUBER 110

    I and Thou
    I-Thou and I-It
    Dialogue
    Distance and Relation
    Elements of the Interhuman
    Ethics and Religion
    Philosophical Anthropology

    Footnotes 150

V. OBSERVATIONS ON BUBER'S POINT OF VIEW . . . 155

    Footnotes 167

VI. CONCLUSION 169

    Footnotes 181

BIBLIOGRAPHY 183

ABBREVIATIONS OF WORKS MOST FREQUENTLY CITED

1. Sartre

    EN   L'Etre et le néant

    BN   Being and Nothingness

    CRD Critique de la raison dialectique

2. Buber

    IT   I and Thou

    BMM Between Man and Man

    KM   The Knowledge of Man

    PMB The Philosophy of Martin Buber

Note: Full references can be found in the Bibliography. In all quotations I have standardized quotation marks to coincide with the following usage: double quotation marks indicate that a special sense is intended for the term; single quotation marks indicate that the term is only being mentioned.

ACKNOWLEDGMENTS

I should like to thank the publishers of the following works for their kind permission to quote extensively from the listed sources:

Buber, Martin. BETWEEN MAN AND MAN. Translated by R.G. Smith, Afterword translated by Maurice Friedman (Copyright © 1965, Macmillan Publishing Co., Inc.)

_____ECLIPSE OF GOD. Translated by Maurice Friedman. (Copyright © 1957, Harper and Row, Publishers, Inc.)

Catalano, Joseph. A COMMENTARY ON JEAN-PAUL SARTRE'S "BEING AND NOTHINGNESS." (Copyright © 1973, Harper and Row, Publishers, Inc.)

Greene, Marjorie. SARTRE. (Copyright© 1973, Franklin Watts, Inc.)

Ryle, Gilbert, THE CONCEPT OF MIND. (Copyright © 1949, Barnes & Noble Books.)

Sartre, Jean-Paul. L'ETRE ET LE NEANT. 1943, Editions Gallimard.)

INTRODUCTION

After a brief sketch of the history of the concept of the Other, this inquiry will examine the ontological structures of the self and the Other as found in the writings of Martin Buber and Jean-Paul Sartre. In addition, various comments by critics on the relative merits of these writers' views will be analyzed in order to determine how tenable certain notions are. Finally, an attempt will be made to compare and contrast the theories of Buber and Sartre not only with respect to their ontology, but also in awareness of problems which arise from the adoption of their positions.

The subject of interpersonal relations, when studied by psychologists, sociologists, anthropologists, educators and psychotherapists, is often examined from the point of view of the specialist, who observes and comments on the manner in which two or more people interact. In such studies, the Other can be any one of the persons under observation. In fact, they are *all* "others." Philosophers who address this problem recognize that as a category, the Other can hold interest only in relation to a *self*--that self who is conscious of his relation to the Other. The self need not be fully cognizant of the effect which each person has upon the other person, but neither can the *selves* and *others* be interchangeable so that the study focuses only on a generalized abstraction of man. Philosophical examination of this topic requires that the Other be viewed in relation to a *particular* self who affects and is affected by the Other.[1]

There are several contexts of philosophy in which the Other can be analyzed. For example, the study can be conducted as a metaphysical inquiry into the ultimate reality of the Other: what is he, who is he, and how did he evolve . . . who and what am I, since in relation to my fellow man, *I* am the Other . . . do the Other and I have a specific purpose in life? Questions of this type can be posited without any value judgments expressed or implied. Nor is it obligatory to inquire into the limits of human ability to know and comprehend the possible answers to such questions.

To be sure, significant problems can be raised in the epistemological and ethical aspects of the concept of the Other. Should solipsism be avoided and, if so, why and how? Is the Other only the person encountered in concrete reality now, or is he also the person in generations to come who will be affected by decisions made now? If the Other is ontologically a threat to my safety and survival, am I not justified in "doing unto him before he does unto me?"

In the study of interpersonal relations, metaphysical, epistemological and ethical considerations all play an important role. It is a vast area of investigation, and it is being explored today as never before. How one views the Other is necessarily an important element in these studies. However, the concept of the relation to the Other is not synonymous with the concept of interpersonal relations, and it is the Other which will be the focus of this work.

Why Buber and Sartre, one may ask? If contemporary philosophers are addressing the problem in increasing numbers, why not study their work, which no doubt incorporates much of Sartre and Buber? And if current theory is _not_ the subject, why select _these two_ writers from the large group of thinkers who have undertaken philosophical explorations of the concept of the Other?

There are several answers to each of these questions. Current theorists are building on the principles of Sartre and Buber, often without knowing very much about them. They use their language, adopt their neologisms, parrot phrases and ideas, but frequently reveal that they have completely misread the philosopher whom they are quoting. There have evolved in the past few decades cults of "Buberians" and "Sartreans" who more often than not are inept in their interpretations of the ideas of their masters.

Why Sartre and not Hegel or Husserl? Why Buber and not Kierkegaard or Heidegger? Both Sartre and Buber assimilated insights of their predecessors and contemporaries into their own work. Moreover, they are both original, in that they pioneered new ways of approaching the same problem. There is more in the philosophy of Sartre than the accumulation of wisdom derived from the study of Descartes, Kant, Hegel, Husserl and Heidegger, although Sartre certainly has profited from the study of all of these thinkers. Grene says that, unlike so many original philosophers who have often been bad historians,

> He *is* an exception. He does use the thinkers of the past (and present) for his own ends, but at the same time he sees them with extraordinary clarity. In references, say, to Kant or Spinoza, he not only uses their thought as a springboard for his own, but also exhibits a solid and scholarly penetration into their principles and views.[2]

Similarly, there is much more to the philosophy of Buber than the Judaic tradition wedded to his encyclopedic knowledge of philosophy in general.

The two men provide an interesting contrast. Influenced by distinct and diverse sources, it is to be expected that they should be poles apart on many issues. Sartre was an atheist. Buber was deeply religious. Sartre sees all relations between men as conflict situations. He characterizes these as a struggle for dominance. "Objectify the Other," he says in many variations, "before he objectifies you. If it is too late, objectify him anyway so that you may regain your freedom." Man is a useless, absurd passion, Sartre writes. We are brought into a contingent world, and no matter what attitude we may adopt toward one another, all relations are doomed to failure. In contrast, Buber was optimistic, encouraging. The life of dialogue cannot be ordered, he said. "It is not that you *are* to answer but that you *are able*."[3] Accused of being a "romantic optimist" by a critic, Buber conceded that it was understandable that he should be identified as such because,

> despite all adverse experiences, I have always clung to the messianic belief in the redemption of the world by God with the participation of the world. But it is quite false; for I have never and nowhere asserted that man can overcome his disharmony, the inner conflict of human existence through his own fullness of power, through his own "good will." I am a realistic meliorist; for I mean and say that human life approaches its fulfillment, its redemption in the measure that the I-Thou relation becomes strong in it, the relation in which man, without surrendering his self-relatedness, has to do with the other not as with his object, but as with his partner.[4]

It should be noted that Sartre and Buber expressed themselves in idiosyncratic styles and they approached the study of philosophy from entirely different backgrounds. Moreover, whereas Sartre declared that *Being and Nothingness* was an essay in phenomenological ontology, and proceeded to write about the self and the Other employing a unique phenomenological style, Buber's ideas have to be gathered from his many writings on religion, ethics, philosophical anthropology, and psychotherapy.[5] Both writers were prolific: they wrote novels, short stories, plays, essays, etc., in addition to their philosophical works. Their literary writings are therefore a fertile source of illustrative material, of amplification of philosophical claims, and of corroboration or refutation of points of view imputed to them.

There is still another advantage in selecting Sartre and Buber, and that arises out of the aforementioned cults that have developed around them. Because of their following and influence some excellent commentaries have been written on the works of both writers. Astute observations, persuasive criticism, lucid elaborations abound in the volumes that have been published on the subject of Buber's philosophy of dialogue and of Sartre's brand of existentialism. In the course of the present study every attempt will be made to include these commentaries, which will amplify and draw attention to the strengths and weaknesses of the views of both authors.

A complete, detailed, historical study of the concept of the Other would adduce not only the sources of the ideas of Sartre and Buber but also their divergence from other writers on this topic. An elaborate historical investigation, however, would detract from the main focus of this study. Therefore, the first chapter will be limited to writers who have contributed to the concept of the Other insofar as they influenced Buber and Sartre. Also, an effort will be made to examine only that aspect of these writers' contributions which refers directly to this concept.

A good deal of exposition will be required in order that the critical comments, the comparisons and a final evaluation may be made. It cannot be presumed that the terms used by each of the writers are self-explanatory, or that their significance can be gleaned from some sort of glossary. It is the <u>concept</u> of the Other that will be investigated, and the singular approaches of Sartre and Buber necessitate a patient, careful exposition of key components in this complex problem. Critical remarks may find their way into the sections of this work which are meant merely to set forth and explain the contention of one or another author, but for the most part, such remarks will be postponed until the expository section is completed.

The critique will be carried out on several levels. Certain questions will be raised about specific issues within one author's interpretation of a particular point. On this level, there is ample critical literature which facilitates the task of pinpointing dubious premises and conclusions. On another level, claims by each writer on the same issue(s) will be compared, without necessarily attempting to find the one right and the other wrong. Finally, the philosophy of Sartre will be compared and contrasted with that of Buber from a wider perspective, making it possible for the concept of the Other to be understood within the context of the total work of both writers.

Footnotes

1. It is convenient for the philosopher to assume the role, as paradigm, of one partner in the relation. The other partner, then, is the one who is designated as the Other.

2. Marjorie Grene, *Sartre* (New York: Franklin Watts, 1973), p. 33.

3. Martin Buber, "Dialogue," in *Between Man and Man* (Henceforth, BMM),(New York: Macmillan Co., 1965), p. 35.

4. Quoted in Sidney and Beatrice Rome, eds., *Philosophical Interrogations* (New York: Holt, Rinehart & Winston, 1964), p. 117.

5. Buber often denied that he "wrote philosophy." He said, "I have no teaching. I only point to something. I point to reality. I point to something in reality that had not or had too little been seen. I take him who listens to me by the hand and lead him to the window. I open the window and point to what is outside . . . I have no teaching, but I carry on a conversation." Martin Buber, "Replies to my Critics," trans. Maurice Friedman, in *The Philosophy of Martin Buber*, ed. Paul Arthur Schilpp and Maurice Friedmand (LaSalle, Illinois: Open Court Press, 1967). p. 693, (Hereafter PMB).

PART ONE

CHAPTER I

HISTORICAL BACKGROUND OF THE CONCEPT OF THE OTHER

A knowledge of the history of the concept of the Other is needed in order to better understand the notions of Sartre and Buber on this subject. It was not always named "the Other", and therefore, the area of investigation has to be extended so as to discover the related concepts which could have been so labeled. For example, in writing about man, a number of writers have assumed that whatever they said about the self applied as well to any other person, whether in relation to this self or not, since, they reasoned, the other person could also be identified with his own self. Other writers have contended that the self more or less invents or "creates" those around it, and therefore limited themselves to explanations of the self.[1]

The problem of interpersonal relations is relatively new to serious studies in philosophy. Emmanuel Mounier has observed that:

> Classical philosophy used to leave it strangely alone. If you enumerate the major problems dealt with by classical philosophy, you have knowledge, the outside world, myself, the soul and the body, the mind, God, and the future life--the problem created by association with other people never assumes in classical philosophy the same importance as other problems.[2]

Mounier was right and wrong. He was right in his claim that "Classical philosophy" did not consider the problem of interpersonal relations to be as important as those which he enumerates above. But he is wrong in overlooking Aristotle's careful commentary on friendship, which certainly indicates the author's concern with this issue.

It would seem that if a writer does not consider the Other a a category separate from that of self, he makes a statement, by his silence, that there is no need to do so. Thus, in almost every philosophical discussion about persons there is an implicit, if not explicit, point of view as to the Other. Besides, relations between persons were never totally ignored. At various epochs in the history of thought, there have been philosophers who appear to have been struck by the relevance of this problem to any discussion about man. In tracing the history of the dialogical principle, (BMM 209), Buber mentions Jacobi and Feuerbach as precursors, but it is apparent from his writings that he was deeply influenced also by Meister Eckhart and Jacob Boehme.[3]

Perhaps the most important influence on Sartre was Descartes,[4] in whose philosophy the problem of the Other is addressed in a systematic way. Kant, as will be shown, investigated certain issues which are tangential to the Other, but these are more significant for what they fail to address than for what they do address. It was not until Hegel that the concept of the Other assumed the prominence which it has held ever since.

In the late nineteenth and in the twentieth century, interest in the concept of the Other has increased steadily. Today, it is the object of numerous studies in philosophy, theology, cognitive psychology, psychotherapy, cultural anthropology, and sociology. These studies are being conducted especially on the continent, but substantial research is in progress wherever there is interest in phenomenology, existentialism, philosophical anthropology, philosophy of mind, etc. For example, in 1956, philosophers from all corners of the world assembled in Toulouse for a conference on the theme of "L'Homme et son prochain" (Man and his fellow-man). So many scholars in diverse disciplines are examining the concept of the Other that it has become impossible to classify the schools accurately and to provide a comprehensive background. Therefore, the section which follows, as stated earlier, will present only the major thinkers whose ideas have directly influenced Sartre and Buber.

The implicit point of view on the Other, mentioned above, is frequently one in which the self is separated from the "outside" world. According to this view the <u>world</u> is <u>outside</u> the consciousness of the person. It was Descartes who described a person's consciousness as distinct in every way from corporeal substance. His second <u>Meditation</u> ends with the conclusion that

> It is now manifest to me that even bodies are not, properly speaking, known by the senses or by the faculty of imagination, but by the understanding only, and since they are not known from the fact that they are seen or touched, but only because they are understood, I see clearly that there is nothing which is easier for me to know than my mind.[5]

According to Descartes, extended things can be known only through inference or deduction. Sensations, although often associated with the objects which usually accompany them, are not conveyed by the objects.[6] They are, rather, projected outward by the consciousness of the perceiver. This theory holds that in an individual's apprehension of his fellow men, it is by means of inference that he judges them to be what they are. The celebrated passage in which Descartes makes this clear is worth noting again:

> ... when looking from a window and saying I

see men who pass in the street, I really do not see them, but infer that what I see is men, just as I say I see wax. And yet what do I see from the window but hats and coats which may cover automatic machines? Yet I judge these to be men. And similarly, solely by the faculty of judgment which rests in my mind, I comprehend that which I believed I saw with my eyes.[7]

In distinguishing men from other creatures Descartes stressed that the faculty of speech is of utmost relevance. However, he held that language originates in thinking substance, and not in one's body. True, it is voiced by means of the body, but the body is no more than an instrument. There is another, very important function served by the body in the Cartesian system: it provides a means whereby the self can apprehend other bodies.

If Descartes succeeded in extricating himself from the charge of solipsism, it was only by a process of reasoning, the veracity of which God was alleged to guarantee. The argument begins with the observation that just as I, a thinking substance, manifest my thoughts by means of a body which is capable of creating language and performing various other activities, so too, when I observe the body of an Other, uttering words which are similar to mine, I can infer that the Other is, as am I, a thinking substance. Moreover, it can be inferred that the Other is the seat of "universal reason," forming, with the rest of men, what can safely be assumed to be a society of men who share in the "community of reason."[8]

Thus, the view that an individual comes to know the Other as a person (in contrast to our apprehending him as an object) by analogy, has its origin in the writings of Descartes. And although the author never designated his notion, 'reasoning by analogy', he described it exactly as such.

According to Laín Entralgo, it was John Stuart Mill who articulated the view that a person apprehends an Other by analogy. In his <u>Examination of Sir W. Hamilton's Philosophy</u>, Mill writes,

> The experience which a person has of himself shows the existence of a causal relation between the following three terms: modification of one's own body, feeling, and expressive appearance. To this experience is added that which is acquired in confronting the body of another person, which is composed of only the first and third components. Now, then, since this body is similar to mine, I must infer by analogy the existence of the second term, and attribute feelings like mine to the corporeal reality which I see before me.[9]

It is evident that whether or not they expressed their views explicitly on the matter, Descartes, Hume, Mill, and numerous other writers believed that a person apprehends an Other by a process of analogy. This notion presents problems, not the least of which is the charge that it is solipsistic. Another problem is that it does not recognize the possibility of the Other's involvement in one's apprehension of oneself.

According to Buber, Kant considered the question, "what is man," to be of paramount importance.[10] In distinguishing universal philosophy from scholastic philosophy, Kant defines the former as "the knowledge of the ultimate aims of human reason," and proposed the following four questions as a starting point for the elaboration of these ultimate aims: "1. What can I know? 2. What ought I to do? 3. What may I hope? 4. What is man?" Further, Kant stated, metaphysics answers the first question, ethics, the second, religion, the third, and (philosophical) anthropology, the fourth. Finally, he concluded, "Fundamentally, all this could be reckoned as [philosophical] anthropology since the first three questions are related to the last" (BMM 119).

To be sure, Kant made many interesting observations on psychology in his lectures on man which he delivered at various times in his career. But he failed to address the question, "What is man?" from the vantage point of the related problems on which so many later writers were to comment. Buber enumerates some of these as follows,

> ...man's special place in the cosmos, his connection with destiny, his relation to the world of things, his understanding of his fellow-men, his existence as a being that knows it must die, his attitude in all the ordinary and extraordinary encounters with the mystery with which his life is shot through, and so on....

and he adds that not one of these problems is seriously touched upon by Kant (BMM 120).

As mentioned before, however, in every discussion about human beings, there is an implicit point of view as to the Other. In the epistemology of Kant the Other can be known only as a phenomenon. The noumenal self, the Other's as well as my own, can never be apprehended. My imagination prompts me to suppose that as a noumenon man is free from physical determinants. My practical reason enables me to abstract from the phenomenal characteristics of a moral action "the concept of a timeless universal moral law which is the ground (not the cause) of the action."[11] But there is, otherwise, very little that can be said positively about man as a thing-in-himself. At best we specify all the things which a noumenon is not, by expressing what can be apprehended by means of the _a priori_ forms of sensibility and the categories.

Man as phenomenon can be studied by the natural sciences. He is not empirically as free as one might suppose. As a matter of fact, Kant says, his physical actions can be calculated with as much precision as the eclipses of the moon. The self, the "I," Kant describes as

> the simple, and in-itself completely empty, representation "I"; and we cannot even say that this is a concept, but only that it is a bare consciousness which accompanies all concepts. Through this I or he or it (the thing) which thinks, nothing further is represented than a transcendental subject of the thoughts = X.[12]

Evidently, the Other has no more personality than the "I," according to this view. And vice versa. Humanity, whom we are enjoined to treat, both in our person in that of every other, always at the same time as an end, and never simply as a means,[13] is essentially the personality of noumenal human beings. It is the person-in-himself, as ground of the appearance, who adheres to the moral law and, more than that, whose will brings the moral law into existence. It is the person-in-himself, as the reality whose phenomenon is so simple and empty, who has a duty to better himself no matter how evil he may have been "up to the very moment of an impending free act."[14]

Indeed, there is in Kant much valuable information on psychology, fertile ground for the nurture of ethical theories, some interesting points on religion, a good deal of metaphysical speculation, but Buber's criticism is well taken: there is not, in all the works of Kant, a real attempt to answer the question, "What is man?".

In the nineteenth century, writers began to distinguish not only between self and otherness but also between the I and the Other. Hegel, it is generally agreed, made a significant contribution to the clarification of the problem. Fichte had declared, "The consciousness of the individual is necessarily accompanied by that of another, that of a Thou, and only under this condition possible" (BMM

209). And Jacobi had written, "The source of all certainty, you are and I am! . . . The I is impossible without the Thou" (BMM 209). But it was Hegel who undertook to describe in philosophical terms the ontological structure of intersubjective relations. In the Encyclopedia he describes self-consciousness as,

> . . . the truth of consciousness: the latter is a consequence of the former, all consciousness of an other object being as a matter of fact also self-consciousness. The object is my idea: I am aware of the object as mine; and thus in it I am aware of me. The formula of self-consciousness is I = I: --abstract freedom, pure 'Ideality'; and thus it lacks 'reality': for as it is its own object, there is strictly speaking no object, because there is no distinction between it and the object.[15]

The Other is the mediator. He appears with me, since consciousness of self is identical with itself only by excluding otherness. In the Zusätze of §430, Hegel explains that the second stage in the development of self-consciousness, namely the process of recognition, continues to have the determination of immediacy in common with the self-consciousness of the first stage. In this determination there is a contradiction that on the one hand the ego is wholly universal (the universal essence common to all men), unconstrained by any limit, absolutely pervasive--and in this sense, two mutually related selves constitute one identity. On the other hand, each of the selves exists as a reflection-in-itself, as totally distinct from the other. Sartre was to appropriate this notion in order to provide the "negation of internality" for his own ontology: "No external nothingness-in-itself separates my consciousness from that of another, but by the very fact that I am I is the other excluded: the Other is what excludes me by being himself, what I exclude by being myself."[16] Sartre credits Hegel with grasping the subtlety of this problem more clearly than Husserl.

The contradiction can be resolved only if an individual recognizes that in his immediate corporeal existence he is also a being-for-others, and still maintains his freedom. If the Other, who "shares" in my identity the essence common to all men, is not totally free, then I cannot be free either. Thus it is freedom which unites men by internal negation. The problem with this notion is that men, existing bodily in the immediate world, are isolated. For a man himself to know that he is free is not enough. He must prove it to himself. And to do that he must disregard the knowledge of his own freedom. Hegel says:

> The fight of recognition is a life and death struggle: either self-consciousness imperils the other's life, and incurs a like peril for its own--but only peril, for either is no less bent on maintaining his life, as the existence of his freedom.[17]

A person, then, must demonstrate to himself that he is not immersed in the world of objectivity. He must be careful, above all, to prove that he is not dependent on the objectivity most closely identifiable with him, i.e., his bodily existence. He must literally **risk** his life, and take a chance that his body will perish. Similarly, he puts the Other to the same test. If the Other is really free, he too will be willing to take a chance in the life-or-death struggle that may ensue.

The two consciousnesses, each willing to face its own death, are proof to one another of the freedom of the self. The two "freedoms" are pitted against each other in a struggle which is complicated by another factor. Admitted, giving up life would prove one's freedom, but there is a force in each of us which directs us toward self-preservation, and this force is opposed to that which drives us to prove our freedom.

Therefore, renouncing life cannot be the manner in which to obtain freedom. One must stand his ground and establish a relationship with the other wherein each person would recognize his own freedom in the actions of the Other.[18]

Human existence is such, however, that given a group of consciousnesses in which each tries to assert its freedom by finding recognition in the Other, there will be some self-consciousnesses which give recognition to the freedom of the others, without receiving it for their own. In other words, the struggle is resolved when one person chooses freedom over life, while the other prefers to "live" and sacrifice his freedom. This is the basis of the master-slave relationship which Hegel described and explained on several occasions.[19] In the *Encyclopedia*, he puts it most succinctly:

> But because life is as requisite as liberty to the solution, the fight ends in the first instance as a one-sided negation with inequality. While the one combatant prefers life, retains his single self-consciousness, but surrenders his claim for recognition, the other holds fast to his self-assertion and is recognized by the former as his superior. Thus arises the status of master and slave.[20]

In this relation neither the master nor the slave achieves his aim of asserting his freedom through the Other. This fact is more evident in regard to the slave, who, according to Hegel, is overcome internally by absolute fear of death. If it were not for the opportunity to negate this fear by meeting the demand of the master (through work) the fear would be paralyzing. Instead, he overcomes it, but in so doing finds his self-consciousness objectified. In obeying his master the slave negates his own essence and forfeits his own will. What remains is absolute negation, pure being-in-itself. Paradoxically, as the slave works to satisfy the wants of the master and not to gratify his own appetite, he rises above the level of selfishness which characterizes the master. On the other hand, the master, in making the slave work and rework the products of the world, thus enjoying the fruit of the efforts of the slave, begins to contemplate him as an object, and not as an other self-consciousness. Since the "common essence" is lacking, the master can no longer find a reflection of his own self-consciousness in the slave. The relationship, therefore, is one which aims constantly at its own reversal. As one commentator explains it,

> Thus the Slave, without starting out from the certainty of free self-consciousness, continually produces the truth of free self-consciousness, along with the possibility of concomitant certitude; while the Master, starting out from this certainty, produces the mere semblance of freedom and self-consciousness, without actually attaining to its objective truth.[21]

So long as the Master-Slave relationship persists, each of the subjects is reflected in the Other--who is not free. Following the transitions which Hegel develops from this apparent impasse, i.e., the transition of Stoicism, from there to Scepticism, and from there to the Unhappy Consciousness, the subject ultimately begins to affirm his will as the universal will. In the end then, there emerges a self-consciousness which is universal. Each person identifies with the Other in a kind of generalized consciousness. When a person reaches the point at which he realizes the truth that consciousness *is* reality, he has attained reason, which itself is a generic category from which other categories can be deduced.[22]

There are probably as many critics of Hegel as there are writers who have attempted to interpret his works. Notably, Sartre found several flaws in the development of the dialectic whereby self-consciousness becomes consciousness, and attacked what he considered to be the "epistemological optimism" of

Hegel. The examination of the points raised by Sartre will be postponed, however, to the section in which his own solutions of the alleged problems will be analyzed. Buber's comments are worth noting also, and they will be. Meantime, his observation about the influence of Hegel may summarize the effect of Hegel on the manner in which the Other has come to be understood. He said, "The Hegelian house of the universe is admired, explained, and imitated; but it proves uninhabitable. Thought confirms it and the word glorifies it; but the real man does not set foot in it" (BMM 140). The image of the universe which Hegel depicted had a widespread effect on philosophy for a century, but the rebellion against it started immediately.

Of the many "young Hegelians" who rebelled against the radical notion of making universal reason the object of philosophy, Feuerbach stands out as the one whose attack was most relevant to our study. In his *Principles of the Philosophy of the Future*, he proclaimed that the new philosophy has as its principle, "not the absolute, that is, the abstract, spirit--in short, not reason *in abstracto*--but man's real, whole being . . . The new philosophy . . . makes man . . . the exclusive, universal . . . object of philosophy, and thus makes anthropology . . . the universal science."[23]

Feuerbach attempted to redirect philosophical thinking toward an understanding of man. As noted, Hegel had already shown that the ego needs a mediator in order to recognize itself (by excluding otherness). Feuerbach emphasized the uniqueness of the Thou as the mediator, i.e., the relation of an I to a Thou as paradigmatic of human consciousness recognizing itself through the Other. But his project of elevating man to be the exclusive focal point of philosophy was even more ambitious.

In his dissertation, "de ratione, una, universali, infinita . . . ." Feuerbach introduced his "discovery" of the species concept (*Gattungsbegriff*) and of man's essence as "species being" (Gattungswesen). The Thou which enables man to identify with himself is not merely another individual, on this account, but rather a universal. The Thou is man's own essence, and thus in the Other we come to identify with all mankind. An important feature of our recognition of universality is that we achieve it by, and it is consumated in, our act of thought. For in thinking we not only express our species nature, we realize it as well.

When an individual is thinking, Feuerbach holds, he is in unity with the object of his thought, the Other, which is a Thou. The Other is only apparently "other" (the same essence as the thought activity of the subject). Here again one sees a model for Sartre's notion of the internal relation which characterizes the self and the Other. But for Feuerbach, any and all Others are one. The author's own words express his position very clearly:

> What I think is, of course, my thought. But it can be separated from me in such a way as to become the entire individual property of another, because if it is taken up by another, it must still be newly brought forth by him. . . . And thus, in general, in every relation of man to man, the other may be called another self. However in thinking, the other is in myself. I am at the same time I and Thou--not any determinate particular Thou, however, but Thou in general, as a species . . .[24]

Though he revised some of his formulations in later writings, Feuerbach was apparently unable to overcome the difficulties inherent in his philosophical stance. For example, to speak of a relation between an I and a Thou, when these are one essence (as the author contended) presents an insuperable problem. Not only does it make no sense to speak of such a relation, but somehow man as a species appears to dissipate into into a vague, universal, Hegelian conception of Reason.

Martin Buber, who at the age of eighteen enrolled at the University of Vienna, studied under F. Jodl, editor of Feuerbach's collected works. The young man's thinking was given a "decisive impetus" by the writings of Feuerbach. Primarily, Buber was inspired by the repositioning of the whole man at the center of the philosophical enterprise, in opposition to Kant and Hegel who had concentrated on human cognition. Moreover, Buber's own philosophical anthropology was to adopt as its central theme the relation between man and man, and his dissertation dealt with the relation between unity and multiplicity. The inspiration of Feuerbach notwithstanding, Buber speaks condescendingly about his predecessor's system. "Instead of logically concluding, 'The unity of I and Thou is a man in the true sense'," says Buber, "he introduces a pseudomystical construction that neither himself nor anyone after him could fill with genuine content" (BMM 210).

At the University of Berlin, at the turn of the century, Buber studied under another philosophy professor who, at the time, had achieved considerable fame. Wilhelm Dilthey had proclaimed that heretofore, philosophy had been dominated by the study of problems presented by natural science and mathematics. He proposed to rectify the situation by developing a Critique of Historical Reason,[25] a study of man in society and history, which would probe the other half of the philosophical enterprise. This type of study was to be wholly different. About it, Hodges writes:

> Instead of observing our object directly, we have to approach it indirectly through written testimony and other similar evidence; instead of clearly formulated theories which can be tested by experiment, we have an attempt to analyze and describe the concrete complexities of life; instead of explanation of particular events and processes through general laws, we have an appreciative

understanding of the meaning and value of the unique individual.[26]

Dilthey's theory of knowledge, in opposition to Kant's, denied any and all a priori concepts. It is in experience that thought processes begin and end. There are no essences, no transcendental selves, there are only human beings living their lives in relation and interaction with their physical environments and social and cultural milieux.[27]

According to Dilthey, life is the "primary reality." The two categories through which this reality is actualized are 1) meaning (<u>Bedeutung</u>) and 2) power (<u>Kraft</u>). Man becomes cognizant of these as constituting the reality of his life through an elemental psychological act, which the author called <u>Erlebnis</u>, or lived experience. As for the overall perspective on life--the manner in which a person perceives and evaluates the world and the way he responds to it--Dilthey called this a Weltanschauung.[28]

Buber, Ortega y Gasset, Heidegger, and a large number of other philosophers, as well as psychologists and sociologists, were deeply influenced by Dilthey. Dilthey convinced his contemporaries that philosophy can be an empirical science, that history must renounce intellectualism (defined by Ortega y Gasset as the "nonhistorical construction of a world by means of pure concepts[29]), and that the understanding of oneself (autognosis) is more fundamental than the understanding of others. To continue to list areas in which the works of Dilthey exerted influence would be as fruitless as to enumerate the concepts and neologisms which the "new" philosophy seems to have adopted from him. It is important, however, to glean from the author's prolific writings precisely how he viewed personality and its relationship with the Other.

In Dilthey's view, we share with other animals such processes as feelings, images, instincts, and volitions--which can be distinguished in our consciousness. Like other animals, human beings generally react to external stimuli in a manner conducive to their preservation and the satisfaction of basic needs. But unlike the lower forms of life, human beings have an internal aspect.

In the objective world we find a certain type of stimulus which differs from the others in that it is alive and apparently volitional. In other words, we meet the Other. Like Descartes, who did not mention analogy but proceeded to write as if it could be taken for granted, Dilthey also reasons by analogy that we attribute more reality to the Other than to inanimate objects, and we strive to understand his experience. At a basic level of understanding I try to imagine what is happening in this unique, interior world.[30]

Dilthey may have influenced a great number of his contemporaries to accept the notion that philosophy can be an empirical science, but it was Edmund Husserl who provided the program for doing so (although the two thinkers meant quite different things by both 'empirical' and 'science'). Phenomenology has undergone many changes since its formulation as a method by Husserl but certain elements of it have persisted and continue to affect the manner in which various philosophical problems are viewed and explicated. Heidegger, Sartre, Buber, Merleau-Ponty, and many other authors who are associated with Existentialism in one way or another, have attempted to provide "phenomenological descriptions" of the objects under investigation.

Husserl proposed that the object of philosophical research should be the experience of consciousness itself. By means of a special type of __reflection__, consciousness could be turned back upon itself, he said, thereby achieving what he called a __reduction__. According to this, the subjective life of a person can reach beyond its subjectivity to the objective structure which makes it possible for consciousness to exist. In other words, the subject can rid himself of assumptions, beliefs, experiences, etc., in order to grasp a reality that is not defined by physical traits. The suspension of these attitudes and judgments was labeled an épouché, or "bracketing", and it was proposed that the reductions could be made in succeeding levels of depth in order to attain <u>pure consciousness</u>. If through the first reduction the thinker can purify his consciousness by suspending his natural beliefs, through a second act of "bracketing" he might uncover the essential forms of experience, the <u>noetic</u> aspect of consciousness. And by pushing further and further into consciousness, Husserl claimed, one could eventually grasp the foundation of the entire world. In his later writings especially, he concentrated more and more on the fundamental reality of being. He had begun by exploring the possibility of experience and ended by endeavoring to discover the essential structure of reality (given the fact that consciousness is able to perceive and experience this structure.)[31]

An important problem which arises from Husserl's program, a problem which the author himself recognized and tried to resolve, is whether or not one can have access to the subjectivity of an Other. Phenomenology, in uncovering the essence of subjectivity, should uncover the essence of more than one person's subjectivity. Husserl realized this, yet insisted, particularly in his earlier writings, that the Other's subjectivity is inaccessible.

To avoid a transcendental solipsism, Husserl asserted that the a priori of consciousness is the same for all subjects. But a subject's experience of an Other is different from his experience of natural objects, since the latter cannot themselves experience the subject reciprocally. The special relationship between two subjects was labeled "sympathy" (<u>Einfühlung</u>) by Husserl, but the account which he set forth for this notion did little more than substitute knowledge of the other by analogy for the previous, solipsistic point of view.[32] Husserl seems to have been aware of this problem too. He went so far as to declare that his account of subjectivity needed elaboration in order to fully explain intersubjectivity, although it must be noted that the author had in mind not concrete, _interpersonal_ relations, but rather an abstract explanation of intersubjectivity as it relates to essences.

Try as he might, Husserl did not succeed in creating a theory which avoids solipsism. His transcendental phenomenology appears to be a complex Monadology. To claim that there is a "single community of monads"[33] does not really solve the problem at all.

Although Husserl's phenomenology may strike a modern reader as being counterintuitive, it should be borne in mind that the numerous authors who subsequently advanced more satisfactory explanations had the benefit of studying Husserl's painstaking investigations. There is no doubt that Sartre and Buber were deeply influenced by the results of these investigations. The _Cartesian_ _Meditations_ served as a springboard of reinterpretations and corrections but also as a provocative source of ideas regarding both the self and the Other.

The aim of discovering foundations rather than establishing a system, declared and carried out by Husserl, was adopted by Max Scheler also. However, whereas Husserl's ambition was to find the underlying ideal essence of all experience, Scheler's interest lay in the _personal_ essence of spirit. As will be indicated below, in the section on Buber's philosophical anthropology, it was Scheler who inspired the emphasis on anthropology, psychology, and sociology which many later thinkers took up in their own philosophical investigations.

In his major work on ethics,[34] Scheler was critical of Kant's approach, which reduced the person to a principle while claiming to consider man always as an end and not as a means. Scheler's phenomenology was intended to shy away from formalism and instead to seek the unity of _act_ and _meaning_ which characterizes a human being. A personal act, according to Scheler, is a spiritual event which synthesizes subject and world in the meaningful order of intentionality.[35] Man is capable of grasping ethical values, and acting on them, because he can move outward from his subjective depth to the meaning and value of objects, and especially of other persons.

This is not the place for a critical discussion of Scheler's view on feeling, love, and religion, although, tangentially, these would amplify the historical account of the concept of the Other. As Dilthey and Husserl had done before him, Scheler gave a new direction not only to the manner of conceptualizing the relation between the self and the Other but also to the methodological approach for the investigation of the problem. And, similarly, as was the case with his predecessors, there were definite periods within the writer's lifetime when views were abandoned or replaced, emphases were changed, etc. In his work, **Man's Place in Nature**,[36] for example, Scheler explored the unconscious elements of the self. In **The Nature of Sympathy**,[37] the focus shifted to the notion of solidarity among all human beings. It is in this latter book that the author expressed his vision of genuine sympathy (*Mitgefühl*) as a guiding principle of man.

Scheler believed that it was possible for one person to have direct knowledge of an Other through participation in the Other's personal act. Such participation was termed--following Dilthey--*understanding* (*verstehen*). This notion, like so many of Scheler's ideas, found its way into the phenomenology of many other writers.

As the concept of the Other gained prominence in the beginning of the twentieth century, and as increasing numbers of authors addressed the problem, it became correspondingly difficult to trace its *historical* development. The study at this point requires a synchronic rather than a diachronic approach, and this will be attempted as the ontologies of Sartre and Buber are examined in detail. However, there is one more author, Heidegger, whose ideas on the self and the Other were so influential that at least a brief mention of his work is vital at this point.

Heidegger's aim, particularly in his early writings, was to rediscover Being by means of an analysis of human being (through which Being reveals itself). Individual, concrete man as he relates to an Other is not as important in Heidegger's account as is man in relation to his own being and his understanding of it--for example, his own death, or his freedom. It should be remembered that Heidegger's goal was to develop a "fundamental ontology," not a philosophical anthropology or a metaphysics. Nevertheless, it would be wrong to assume that Heidegger advocates an interpretation of <u>Dasein</u> as a purely objective consciousness through which Being is disclosed. Since human being reaches out beyond itself to the world, it is relational. It is, indeed, a being-in-the world.[38]

An examination of the concepts of transcendence, "das Man," "zuhanden," and "vorhanden," as explained by Heidegger, would help us to understand his point of view on certain notions which are pertinent in the analysis of the self and the Other. However, a superficial account would create more confusion than clarification, and detailed scrutiny cannot be justified inasmuch as it would divert us from the topic at hand.

The most important structure of being-in-the-world, for purposes of the present study, is "care" (<u>Sorge</u>), interpreted by some writers as "concern." Much more essential than Dasein's relation to things-at-hand is its involvement with other beings. Spatially and temporally, Dasein orients itself in relation to beings which are in turn given a place in the world within the limits thus established by care. Concern for the Other, in Heidegger's ontology, is a necessary structure of being-in-the-world. Such concern, in contrast to the care which Dasein manifests in relation to things-at-hand is characterized by what the author labels _solicitude_. One might expect that this insight would have moved Heidegger to examine precisely the structure of interpersonal relations, but Heidegger was more interested in what he considered to be real, authentic existence. And for self-being to be resolute, i.e., to achieve the highest level, it cannot, indeed it must not, jeopardize its attainment of freedom. In stressing the value of overcoming its identification with "das Man," the crowd, the mass, the anonymity which deprives it of the responsibility to achieve self-being, Heidegger seems to overlook the suggestion of Feuerbach and Scheler that only through a relation with an Other can self-being be achieved.[39]

Heidegger's stance would be more tenable if it were possible to isolate the self from the Other. There is little argument against an ontic view of man which points to the value of "authentic existence," however one may construe the notion of authenticity. The question is: how can a person achieve true self-being, even as Heidegger describes it, through existence which at most provides for the _mere solicitude_ for Others? It is hoped that this question will be answered satisfactorily in the sections which follow.

The historical sketch of the concept of the Other presented in the pages above was not intended to be comprehensive, nor was there any attempt to examine in depth any writer or group of writers. Rather, I have endeavored in this section to provide a kaleidoscopic view of the manner in which the self and the Other have been explained by writers who: (1) had a unique approach to the investigation of the problem, (2) suggested a new way to conceptualize the problem, (3) were noteworthy for their influence on Sartre and Buber, and (4) provided a vocabularly which facilitates the discussion which will follow.

There is no urgent reason to examine Sartre's account before Buber's, nor vice versa. I have chosen to begin with Sartre, as it may be found useful to keep in mind _his_ description of relations in the analysis of Buber's.

Footnotes

1. Laín Entralgo, in his comprehensive study, *Teoría y realidad del Otro*, vol. 1 (Madrid: Revista de Occidente, 1961), has classified philosophers who addressed the problem of the Other as those who considered him to be (1) another "I", (2) the object of an instinctive and feeling "I", (3) a goal of the moral activity of the "I", (4) a member of the dialectic of the mind and of nature, (5) an invention of the "I", and (6) the *alter ego* in Husserl's phenomenological reflection.

2. Emmanuel Mounier, *Existential Philosophies*, trans, Eric Blow (New York: Macmillan Co., 1949), p. 72.

3. e.g., Martin Buber, "Ueber Jacob Boehme," *Wiener Rundschau* V, no. 12 (June 15, 1909): 251-53.

4. In her penetrating book on *Sartre*, p. 35, Grene says "Descartes holds a peculiar position in contrast [to Hegel]. It is a residuum of Cartesian metaphysics which both limits the scope of Sartre's phenomenology and, in large measure, dictates the subject matter as well as the style of his dialectic."

5. René Descartes, *Philosophical Works*, vol. 1, trans. E. S. Haldane and G. R. T. Ross (New York: Dover Publications, 1975), p. 157.

6. Ibid., p. 255.

7. Ibid., pp. 155-56.

8. Entralgo, *Teoría y realidad del Otro*, p. 38.

9. Cited in Entralgo, *Teoría y realidad del Otro*, p. 66. Gilbert Ryle, *The Concept of Mind* (New York: Barnes & Noble, 1949), p. 53, in less elegant language, contends that explanations of this type are not sound, adding, "No one feels happy with the view that for one person to follow what

another person says or does it to make inferences somewhat like those made by a water-diviner from the perceived twitching of the twig to the subterranean flow of water. So the consolatory amendment is sometimes made that, since a person is directly aware of the correlations between his own private experiences and his own overt actions, he can understand the performances of others by imputing to them a similar correlation. Understanding is still psychological divining, but it is divination reinforced by analogies from the diviner's direct observation of the correlations between his own inner and outer lives. But this amendment does not abolish the difficulty."

10. Kant is alleged to have adopted this position in the Handbook to his lectures on logic, which, Buber says, the German philosopher expressly acknowledged, though he himself did not publish it. This, and the information which follows, regarding the Handbook, is contained in Section One of Buber's essay, "What is Man?" in *BMM*, pp. 118f.

11. H. J. Paton, *The Categorical Imperative: A Study in Kant's Moral Philosophy* [1947] (New York: Harper Torchbooks, 1967), p. 270.

12. Immanuel Kant, *Critique of Pure Reason*, trans. Norman Kemp Smith (New York: St. Martin's Press, 1965), (B404).

13. Immanuel Kant, *Groundwork of the Metaphysic of Morals*, trans, H. J. Paton (New York: Harper Torchbooks, 1968), p. 95.

14. Immanuel Kant, *Religion Within the Limits of Reason Alone*, trans. Theodore M. Greene and H. Hudson (New York: Harper Torchbooks, 1960), p. 36.

15. George Wilhelm Friedrich Hegel, *Philosophy of Mind/Part 3 of the Encyclopedia of the Philosophical Science*, trans. William Wallace, together with the Zusätze in Boumann's text, trans. A. V. Miller (Clarendon: Oxford University Press, 1971), 424, p. 165.

16. Jean-Paul Sartre, *L'Etre et le néant*, (hereafter EN) (Paris: Gallimard, 1943), p. 292. English version: *Being and Nothingness*, (hereafter BN), trans. by Hazel Barnes, (New York: Philosophical Library, 1956)

17. Encyclopedia, 432, p. 172.

18. The description by Hegel of what is now often called the intersubjective elements of human relationships clearly indicates that the later explications by Buber and Sartre owe a considerable debt to him.

19. In the *Phenomenology of Mind, Philosophic Propaedeutics*, and in the *Encyclopedia of Philosophical Sciences*.

20. Hegel, Encyclopedia, 433, p. 173

21. Howard P. Kainz, *Hegel's Phenomenology, Part I: Analysis and Commentary* (University, Alabama: The University of Alabama Press, 1976), p. 90.

22. In order to do justice to Hegel's logical development of these ideas, the overview of the history of the concept of the Other would have to be burdened unduly.

23. Quoted in BMM, pp. 146-47.

24. Ludwig Feuerbach, *Dissertation*, in *Collected Works*, ed. W. Bolin and F. Jodl (1903-11), vol. IV, p. 305, cited in Marx W. Wartofsky, *Feuerbach* (Cambridge: Cambridge University Press, 1977), p. 35.

25. Although he created widespread interest in the notion, Dilthey never published the *Critique of Historical Reason*.

26. H. A. Hodges, *The Philosophy of William Dilthey*, (London: Routledge and Kegan Paul, 1944), pp. xiv-xv.

27. Though Buber is know primarily for his analysis of the I-Thou relation, this particular bias of Dilthey's is also one of Buber's most persistently defended views.

28. I am indebted to Rudulf A. Makkreel, whose book *Dilthey* (Princeton: Princeton University Press, 1975), provides a clear and insightful examination of the philosopher's somewhat abstruse writings.

29. José Ortega y Gasset, *Concord and Liberty*, trans, Helene Weyl (New York: W. W. Norton & Co., 1946), p. 176.

30. Laín Entralgo has written that the account of this superior level of understanding is one of the weak points of Dilthey's system since it is founded on our merely *guessing* what the Other thinks and feels. *Teoría y realidad del Otro*, p. 137. Buber claimed, in describing genuine dialogue, that "imagining the real" is a *sine qua non*, (see p. 166 below). The fact is that though conjecturing what the Other feels may be an essential element of true dialogue, it is not sufficient to account for the ontological reality of the Other.

31. I am indebted to Pierre Thevanaz' essay, "What is Phenomenology", in *What is Phenomenology? and Other Essays*, ed. James M. Edie (Chicago: Quadrangle Books), 1962, pp. 37-92 for lucid explanation of some of Husserl's often subtle and difficult ideas.

32. Edmund Husserl, *Cartesian Meditations*, trans. Dorion Cairns (The Hague: Martinus Nijhoff, 1970), pp. 131-36.

33. Ibid., p. 140.

34. Max Scheler, *Der Formalismus in der Ethik und die materiale Wertethik* (Bern: Francke Verlag, 1954).

35. Ibid., pp. 399-400.

36. Max Scheler, *Man's Place in Nature* (New York: Farrar, Straus & Cudahy, 1962).

37. Max Scheler, *The Nature of Sympathy* (New Haven: Yale University Press, 1954).

38. Martin Heidegger, *Vom Wesen des Grundes* (Frankfurt Am Main: Klostermann, 1955), p. 19.

39. Martin Heidegger, *Being and Time*, trans. John Macquarrie and Edward Robinson (New York: Harper & Row, 1962).

PART ONE

CHAPTER II

THE OTHER IN THE ONTOLOGY OF SARTRE

Jean-Paul Sartre was well-acquainted with the writers mentioned in the foregoing historical sketch. Although he was indebted to some of these thinkers for the formulation of his own views, he did not agree with their interpretations of ontology. It was not particularly the concept of the Other with which he took issue, but rather the structure of being, the origin of negation, the human reality within the total scheme--these were the notions he wanted to explain definitively. In writing **Being and Nothingness**, Sartre aimed at providing no less than a phenomenological description of what the title declares. It is within this ambitious scope, and against the confused background of preceding explanations of the Other that the problem at hand must be viewed and examined.

It may be helpful to stop for a moment and consider an abbreviated form of the table of contents of **Being and Nothingness** in order to see how and where Being-for-others fits into the plan. The major divisions of the book are:

Introduction: In Search of Being

Part One: The Problem of Nothingness

Part Two: Being-for-itself

Part Three: Being-for-others

Part Four: Having, Doing, and Being

Conclusion

Obviously, Sartre has not written a work about the Other which presupposes a general acceptance of a notion of the self. Nor is there any attempt on the part of the author to advance any particular ethics regarding the relation between persons. Were it not for the internal relation between persons which characterizes the ontological structure of being-for-others, Sartre might not have devoted as much attention to it as he did. Before describing in a masterly way the psychological effects which people have upon each other, he described minutely the phenomena of self-deception, anguish and guilt which the individual experiences without, as it were, the "help" of others. Human consciousness and its almost limitless freedom was the problem of paramount concern to Sartre.

As noted in the Introduction to the present study, a certain amount of exposition is needed before any significant criticism can be made or reported concerning the ideas of Sartre. One needs to review the vocabulary and the major themes of the author in order to better understand his abstruse account of Being-for-others.[1] The exposition of the first two parts of *Being and Nothingness* and the Introduction will necessarily be sketchy and minimal so that sufficient attention may be devoted to a careful description of the third part, Being-for-others.

In-Itself and For-Itself

According to Sartre, there is not only Being-in-itself, but Nothingness as well. Being is massive, static in its form and time. It does not *ex*ist (stand out). It *is* this desk or that inkstand. Sartre has less to say about it than he does about the "for-itself" which apprehends what-is. The "for-itself" is the consciousness which apprehends that it is not "being-in-itself." By an act of nihilation (néantisation), the for-itself distinguishes itself from being-in-itself and thus gives form to the things that are in the world. If the in-itself were all that there is in the world, there would be no world. There would be a desolate, static landscape devoid of space and time.

It is only by emptying the for-itself that nothing is left, i.e., the in-itself. In Sartre's scheme, the Nothingness is wrested from Being. Consciousness of not-being Peter, or this table, or that idea, ultimately reveals that the for-itself is not really anything that *is*.

Whereas Sartre sets consciousness and thing in opposition to each other, Merleau-Ponty casts doubt on the plausibility of such opposition. He contends, rather, that our consciousness coexists with the "thing," and adds that,

> We understand the "thing" as we understand a new behavior, that is, not by an intellectual classification but by recapturing in our minds the way of existence such as it is outlined by observable signs.[2]

Gilbert Varet raises an important question regarding the limits of representation and supplies an explanation in Sartrean terms when he declares,

> No doubt the most difficult problem of a theory of consciousness is to know why that which is representable is not being represented. Let us recall how, for Sartre, the representation of every "this" is realized by the organization of all those not actually represented, all the other "this" in discreet presence, in "open horizon," - an organization named "world background." The world itself is *nothing* - that is to say that it is entirely "on the side of consciousness," entirely "human", - nothing, that is to say everything which this actual consciousness is justly held to "negate" in order to realize solitary presence, here and now, of the thing-phenomenon.[3]

The commentary on Sartre's notion of the opposition of consciousness and "things" is understandably extensive. It addresses metaphysical issues as well as epistemological difficulties inherent in Sartre's description of how the for-itself separates itself from the in-itself.

The in-itself has no temporality. It cannot be altered or destroyed. There is as much being in the in-itself before it "perishes" as after. Only a human witness, a for-itself, perceives and chooses to conceptualize the ostensible change as "destruction." As Spinoza had pointed out long before, disorganization implies a presupposed organization, and imperfection implies a knowledge of perfection.

The in-itself cannot know. It cannot have desires, feel lack, and thereby create value. It has no connection with time, except that imposed on it by the for-itself. The example which Sartre gives of a green house which has been painted blue, serves as a good illustration. Does it make sense to say that the house *was* green, or *used to be green*? *There is no green house*, says Sartre, except in the memory of a human consciousness. Even the present does not, strictly speaking, apply to the in-itself, for present, to Sartre, means present *to something*. The in-itself merely is.

There are structures of the in-itself which can be and are discussed, but we need to keep in mind constantly that the structures are imposed; they are not inherent in the in-itself. One can speak of *quality*, for the in-self can be said to reveal itself as something which is. One can speak of potentiality, for the human consciousness brings into the world the in-itself with a certain potency. In this respect, the notions of Heidegger on the "*zuhanden*" and "*vorhanden*" are similar to those of Sartre. One can speak of the *usability* of the in-itself, again because of the uses to which the for-itself can put the in-itself.

Knowledge is the connecting link between the in-itself and the for-itself. But, as Husserl pointed out, the intuition (knowledge) is not the presence of a thing to consciousness. On the contrary, it is the presence of a consciousness to the thing. Equally with space, it is the for-itself which notices that this is external to that, or overlaps it, or whatever. So again, by the intervention of the for-itself, the in-itself assumes shape, or, for that matter, being (but certainly not existence!)

As mentioned earlier, the for-itself, as human reality, cannot be properly said to *be*, as *is* the in-itself which is made-to-be through negations of what it is not. Yet human reality is such that one is born at a certain time and place, not having chosen to be born, and not having been consulted as to when, where, to what parents, with what genetic background and physical appearance. These, for Sartre, are the facticities of the for-itself. And, in a manner of speaking, the for-itself, therefore, *is*, i.e., it *is* its faciticity, and facticity is contingent. Contingency is encountered again and again at the basis of Sartrean metaphysics. Consciousness is the cause of its *manner* of being, but nothing is the cause of consciousness (EN 22, n. 1). The for-itself, one must conclude, is contingent both as consciousness and as facticity.

However, the for it-self is more than its body, its past, . . . its facticity. It can never be identified completely with what it *is*, because the for-itself is a *transcendence* also. As we contemplate our facticities, we also assimilate them. We realize that what we are doing in relation to them is but one of many possible ways to behave. Our facticities and transcendences are simultaneous. Thus, we try to transform our transcendence into facticity and our facticity into transcendence,[4] but we cannot succeed in doing so. We are in *bad faith* when we try.

When we lie to others, we keep the truth from them and they are not aware that we are doing so. When we lie to ourselves, we know that we are lying. As Sartre explains it, in **bad faith** the one who lies and the one who believes the lie are one and the same, which means that,

> I must know, as the liar, the "truth" which is hidden from me, as the one who has been deceived. More than that, I must know this truth very precisely _in order to_ hide it from myself more carefully - and this not at two different moments of temporality - which would permit, in a strict sense, reestablishing some semblance of duality - but in the unitary structure of one single project. (EN 87-88)

Consciousness cannot but be consciousness of something, says Sartre, echoing Husserl and Brentano. There is intentionality not only in our actions, but in our awareness as well. By being conscious of what we are not, by a series of negations, we become conscious of what we are. As we are always conscious of something, however, we are not thereby necessarily conscious of being conscious. Only if we concentrate on the fact that we are conscious will we be aware of being conscious. In prereflective consciousness, we concentrate on what we are doing, and not on the fact that we are concentrating.

In a work as ambitious in scope and as meticulous in its attention to subtleties as **Being and Nothingness**, the elaboration of the notions to which I have alluded in the preceding pages, as can be expected, is thorough and epistemologically rigorous. Although Sartre's project is declared to be phenomenological,[5] and throughout the work a certain consistency is observed in the idiosyncratic phenomenological approach of the author, the careful reader is nevertheless aware that Sartre (who was a close student of philosophy, and probably an excellent teacher) was vigilant in investigating the particular area which engaged him. Thus, where he corroborates or contradicts a traditional, or even a peculiar explanation of a certain question, he carefully explains his reasons for doing so. One may not always agree with Sartre's views, but one cannot accuse him of being careless.

Not only are the ideas outlined above presented and explained in great detail in *Being and Nothingness*, but there are numerous others to which I have not even referred. A complete summary of all the sections of *Being and Nothingness* would clutter the present study; worse, it would only duplicate the efforts of other commentators who have already addressed this task.[6] The preceding remarks will suffice, then, to introduce Sartre's vocabulary and metaphysical vantage point as we begin to examine his account of the structures of Being-for-others.

The Existence of the Other

Neither realism nor idealism can provide an account of the Other which Sartre would find satisfactory. They share the presupposition, he claims, that the negation which constitutes the structure of being-the-other is one of exteriority. Husserl, Heidegger, and Hegel are also rejected. In *Being and Nothingness*, Sartre uncovers the alleged weaknesses of the positions of these writers (as will be detailed below) and proceeds to explicate his own point of view in light of the structures of being-in-itself, being-for-itself and being-in-the-world, as he has developed these notions in the preceding sections of his book.

Although he did not find their explanations of the Other totally compatible with his own theory, Sartre did draw heavily from the writings of these thinkers. George L. Kline has pointed out that the basic categories in *Being and Nothingness* are drawn mainly from Hegel's *Phenomenology*, with some additional material taken from the *Logic*.[7] The terms 'being and nothingness', 'in-itself', 'for-itself', 'in-itself-for-itself', to name but those most closely identified with the French author, are Hegelian terms faithfully translated into French. But more than the mere terms is taken over and adapted to the needs of Sartre. The concepts to which the terms refer are also appropriated. And Kline presents strong arguments to support his claim that Sartre "took over not only ideas that were there to be taken, but also at least a few ideas that were not there, or at least were not intended . . . to be taken in the way Sartre took them."[8] Klaus Hartmann's book[9] provides precise documentation and an interpretation of the affinities and differences between the two philosophers' views. It would be foolish to attempt to defend Sartre against the numerous charges that he drew heavily from the early works of Hegel, considering especially the convincing arguments of Kline and Hartmann.[10] It is worth noting also that although Sartre is eager to expose the blind spots of Husserl and Heidegger, he is indebted to these writers, too, perhaps more than he would like to admit.

Realism and idealism, as mentioned earlier, give an unsatisfactory explanation of the existence of the Other, according to Sartre. The realist, in taking everything as given, includes the Other as given also. In the midst of the real, Sartre asks, what can be more real than the Other? (EN p. 277). I perceive the Other as a body. My body is separated from his in space. But the realist does not account for the consciousness of the Other any more than he accounts for mine. He ignores, therefore, the reciprocity of two consciousnesses communicating without the intermediary of the bodies. As Sartre explains it, in the realists's view the Other's soul is separated from mine by the total distance which separates my soul from my body, my body from that of the Other, and the body of the Other from his own soul (EN 277). As for the relation between bodies (this is the simpler example which Sartre chooses as sufficient to discredit realism; but he promises to take up later the more complicated problem of the relation between the for-itself and its own body—and does so), it cannot be anything else than one of pure externality.

The Other's soul does not enter into my intuition of him as a body. Rather, his soul is an absence. It is strange, Sartre declares, that realism, which is founded on intuition, does not account for the intuition of the soul of the Other—which means that it does not provide for the intuition of the Other (EN 278). To be sure, the body which one intuits is the body _of_ _a_ _person_, and is an integral part of one's concept of a person, but realism destroys the body since it does not integrate it in its human totality. It dispenses with the body as a surgeon kills a piece of malignant tissue by separating it from the totality of the living organism. Besides, in the realist's view, it is not the Other's body which I intuit, but rather _a_ body. (EN 278)

The realist is not concerned with these problems. He uses analogy to explain the nuances of the effects of a consciousness (which is totally foreign to me) upon the Other's body. The analogy rests upon what I know about the relation of _my_ body and _my_ mind. Otherwise, as the positivistic and realistic psychologies of the last century showed us, we can learn to interpret, for example, "the sudden reddening of a face as a sign that blows and furious cries will follow." (EN 278 emphasis mine). Of course, the most that this theory can provide for us is a probable knowledge of the Other. There is no certainty that the Other _is_ _more_ _than_ _a_ _body_. The behaviorists, on this account, might have developed the correct idea. Why not reduce the sum of the reactions on the Other's face (muscular contractions, triggered by neurological impulses whose routes can be traced) to simple or conditioned reflexes? The vast majority of psychologists are convinced that the Other is a reality as "integral" as is their own. It is the knowledge that we have about the Other that is probable—his existence is already a certainty. Here, then, says Sartre, is the point at which we are shown the sophistry of realism. For, if the Other is accessible to us only through our knowledge of him, and if this knowledge is only conjectural, then the existence of the Other is only conjectural also, and it is the role of critical reflection to determine its exact degree of probability. The realist is thus forced to turn to idealism as he ponders the question of the existence of the Other, whose *esse* is a simple *percipi* (if his body is an extended substance acting upon thinking substance). For Sartre, therefore, the "modern" theories of *Einfühlung, sympathy*, and *forms* are but refinements in the method of describing how one makes the Other present (EN 279).

If realism refers us to idealism, if the Other is but "my representation," would it not be better to examine the problem immediately from the perspective of critical idealism? Sartre's rhetorical questions are often followed by unexpected rejoinders. In this instance, we are warned that Kant and his followers cannot offer us much help. Too preoccupied with establishing universal laws of subjectivity, the Kantians, Sartre alleges, neglected to consider the problem of individual persons. The *subject*, for Kant, is an abstraction. It is the common essence of all men, just as the universal laws of subjectivity are the same for all men.

Sartre echoes Buber when he declares that Kant never really addressed the problem of the Other.[11] The idealist might have done so, had he not placed himself at the vantage point of the pure subject in order to determine the conditions of possibility for objects in general and even for categories of objects, e.g., physical objects, mathematical objects, those which present teleological characteristics. Kant should have realized, Sartre says, that, though the Other is given to experience as an object, it is a very particular object. Even so, if it be true that the Other represents a particular type of object which reveals itself to our experience, from the perspective of even a rigorous Kantianism we must inquire how knowledge of the Other is possible.

Sartre rules out the possibility of treating the problem of the Other as similar to that of noumenal realities. It would be quite erroneous to do so, he says, even though one could inquire about the Other's noumenal existence. If it be legitimate to do so about my own, and if the Other be similar to me, it would seem permissible to question the Other's intelligible existence as well as my own. Sartre adds that the conclusion we draw for the one will certainly apply to the other, too. But, he points out, the Other whom I meet in daily experience is not a noumenal Other. He is a phenomenal Other who refers me to other phenomena. His appearance occurs as a presence of organized forms (e.g., gestures, acts) that refer to an organizing unity which is situated outside of my experience. The Other is the synthetic unity of his perceptions. As a will and as a passion he organizes my experience. Therefore, Sartre explains,

> . . . it is not a question of the pure and simple action of an unknowable noumenon upon my sensibility, but of the constitution of connected groups of phenomena within the field of my experience by a being who is not I. (EN 280-81)

We cannot consider the Other as a regulative concept either. In seeking to "bind together" experiences which are not and cannot be my experiences, my efforts at constructing and unifying cannot serve for the unification of my own experience. Granted, says Sartre, ideas like the world, for example, also elude my experience; but at least they are referred back to it and have significance only through it, whereas the Other is the object which I try to determine, but which instead denies my own character as subject and determines me as object. He concludes that, in the idealist's account, the Other can be considered as neither a constitutive nor a regulative concept (EN 283).

There remain but two possible solutions for the Kantian, both of which seem unproductive. One is to abandon completely the concept of the Other (and prove that it is not necessary to the constitution of my experience); the alternative is to affirm the real existence of the Other. If one opts for the first solution, Sartre explains, one thereby chooses solipsism, for one asserts that outside of oneself nothing exists. Even on a more conservative account, were one to cling to the solid ground of one's own experience and avoid making use of the concept of the Other, one would remain on the level of critical positivism, and even then it would derive its justification from the contradictions of the notion of the Other considered in the perspective of idealism.

The other solution, the one which Kant and post-Kantians adopted in order to avoid solipsism, affirms the existence of the Other, but such thinkers justify their affirmation only by referring to our common sense and to our deep-rooted prejudices. The fact is that by assuming this position toward the Other we break out of the idealist framework and are thrown back into metaphysical realism. "By positing a plurality of closed systems which can communicate only through the outside," Sartre declares, "we implicitly reestablish the notion of substance." (EN 284)

To explain the strange inversion whereby realism results in idealism, and idealism, insofar as it attempts to avoid solipsism, results in realism, Sartre points to the presupposition which is common to both doctrines, i.e., that the constituting negation implicit in our awareness of the Other as the **not-I**, is an external negation. And this presupposition, as Hegel had already made clear,[12] is erroneous.

At the point in **Being and Nothingness** where the author, having shown the inadequacy of realism and idealism, could be expected to propose his own solution, there is a further delay. Sartre gives credit to Husserl, Hegel, and Heidegger for having attempted to escape solipsism while maintaining a "fundamental, transcending connection" with the Other. At the same time, however, he declares that these thinkers, though they were on the right track, nevertheless went astray. They maintained that the fundamental connection with the Other is established through knowledge; and that, according to Sartre, is wrong. We have already alluded to the basic theories of these three thinkers and need not do so again except to point out that Sartre's criticism appears to be valid, with regard to Husserl only. Hegel certainly does not establish the fundamental connection with the Other through 'knowledge', and neither does Heidegger.

What is Sartre's position then? How does he analyze and describe the fundamental relation between one person and another? The answers to these questions wil occupy a major portion of the remaining pages of this section. Sartre's theory is complex. His examples, illustrations, and descriptions are copious. And in the rare case wherein these might be lacking, one needs but to consult the author's numerous plays, novels and essays in order to find an abundance of illustrative material. At the end of the analysis one is left with the rather pessimistic conclusion which Garcin articulates near the end of Huis Clos, i.e., "Hell is other people."[13] Before reaching this conclusion, Sartre will have declared that relations between people are basically sadomasochistic. As for the possibility of experiencing the "we," he believes that such an experience could not constitute an ontological structure of human reality.

According to Sartre, for a theory of the existence of others to be valid, it must meet four necessary and sufficient conditions, namely:

1. It must be recognized that the existence of others cannot be proven. "The probability of his existence as Another Self can never be either validated or invalidated; it can neither increase nor decrease,[14] it cannot even be measured. . . ." (EN 307) At best, we can affirm the existence of an Other the way Descartes suggested we affirm our

own existence. We cannot _prove_ that we exist, Sartre contends, but we never cease to practice the _cogito_. Therefore, it is this _cogito_ which must be elucidated.

2. It must be established that we are not seeking reasons for believing that the Other exists, but rather, ". . . the concrete, indubitable presence of a particular, concrete Other . . ." (EN 308)

3. The _cogito_ must reveal to us not the mental representation conforming to the Other (not the Other-as-object) but rather a being who "interests" our being.

4. We must reject the notion that an external negation reveals the Other to me. Instead, my apprehension of the Other must derive from an internal relation, which Sartre defines as ". . . a synthetic, active connection of the two terms, each one of which constitutes itself by denying that it is the other." (EN 309)

It goes without saying that Sartre's theory conforms to these criteria. One is tempted to conjecture that the author may have written the criteria after he had completed the phenomenological description of the structure of Being-for-Others. Otherwise, why posit these four conditions and not more, or different ones? It is not as though Sartre proves conclusively that any other condition would be misleading, superfluous, or contradictory to empirical evidence. Nevertheless, the conditions are explained satisfactorily and the exposition which follows meets them unequivocally. For example, let us consider "the Look."

Sartre's Concept of the Other

The Look

Sartre begins by establishing, in language reminiscent of Descartes, his conviction that the people he sees passing in the street are for him objects. Of that, there is no doubt, he says. At least one of the modalities of the Other's presence to me, then, is "objectness." But if the relation of objectness between the Other and myself were fundamental, his existence would be merely conjectural. However, it is not conjectural but probable that the voices I hear are those of persons and not tape recorders, and that the passersby I encounter are people and not robots. Thus, the progression from the objectness of the Other to the probability of his being a person leads me to infer that the Other, as probable object, refers not to "an original solitude beyond my reach, but to a fundamental connection in which the Other is manifested in some way other than through the knowledge which I have of him." (EN 310) It is this latter relation which is fundamental. In it, the Other is revealed to me as another human consciousness, as a _subject_.

When I walk down the street, I make observations--that car is about fifty feet away from me; I'd better wait until it passes before I attempt to cross. The car coming from the opposite direction is even farther away . . . _from me_. Should a person come within my range of perception, the person too could be observed as having a relation of distance to me. But as the Other approaches, I become aware that in relation _to him_ there are distances that can be measured. If he hesitates before crossing the street, it is because he has judged that the oncoming car poses a threat to _his_ safety. I can never be sure of how he perceives that car, how the objects in his world present themselves to him. But there is a new relation now, ". . . one without parts, given at one stroke inside of which there unfolds a spatiality which is not _my_ spatiality; for instead of a grouping _toward me_ of the objects, there is now an orientation _which flees from me_." (EN 312) I become aware that there is someone who sees as I see, who is a subject in relation to another objectness. As a matter of fact, I recognize that I may be an object in relation to _him_, and I become aware of something in his presence which was not the case before, namely, that I am seen. Thus, the "look" of the Other reveals to me that he is a subject, that he is real. He is no longer conjectural, or merely probable. He exists as the concrete, indubitable presence of a particular, concrete Other."[15]

Nevertheless, according to Sartre, the above does not enable us to abandon completely the level on which the Other is an object. Only in and through the revelation that I am for him "being-as-object," can I apprehend his presence as "being-as-subject." The relation which the author calls "being-seen-by-another," i.e., the "permanent possibility that a subject who sees me may be substituted for the object seen by me, justifies my supposition that the Other is probably a person and not a robot." (EN 315) And since the Other can, for the time being, be identified as the one who looks at me, it becomes very important to explain the philosophical meaning of the Other's look.

Sartre's explanation consists of a series of examples, each of which reinforces the notion that "being seen" does not mean necessarily the "convergence of two ocular globes in my direction." (=BN 257) More often, we are vaguely aware of being seen, for example, when we hear footsteps behind us as we are walking down a dark street late at night, or when we hear the slight opening of a shutter. During a battle soldiers may apprehend as "a look" a frame house at the top of a hill, and that particular "look" must be avoided. We might say that thee examples represent the eye, but, says Sartre, the eye is the support of the "look." Aware of the Other's look, I do not perceive his eyes. To perceive is to look at, the author explains, and to apprehend a look is not to apprehend a look-as-object in the world. It is to be conscious of being looked at (EN 316). The Other's look refers me to my self. The guerilla fighter who hears branches crackling in the bush near him does not think that there is somebody there, he does not stop to locate the eyes of the enemy soldier, he becomes aware that he is vulnerable, that *he is seen*.

Shame

Caught in the act of spying upon others through a keyhole (Sartre's illustration is very vivid), I become immediately and prereflectively aware of myself as I apprehend that *I* am an object for *another*. Whereas a moment before, as I spied on their activities through the keyhole, there were others whose freedom I had "captured," it is now I whose freedom and transcendence have dissipated. My jealousy, now that I have been caught, is transformed into shame. So long as it was I who transcended the situation, there was no identification of myself with my jealousy. But to the Other, I am the person who was spying through a keyhole, the person who is jealous.

The Other reveals to me that my possibilities have an external aspect of which I can be made aware only through him. The Other's look fixes me within a certain space and time. It informs me that *my* freedom is challenged by *his* freedom. As Catalano puts it:

> . . . not only is my transcendence transcended, but my spatializing and temporalizing are spatialized and temporalized. . . . Further, only through the other-as-subject can I be revealed as having a self that is a myself, that is, a self that is not the self of the other. Thus, within the cogito, I experience the other as a fact that cannot be deduced from my own consciousness; I experience the other as an essential modification of my own consciousness. The other is not first *perceived* in the world; rather, he is first experienced as the alienation of our possibilities and the objectiveness of ourselves.[16]

Before the Other, I recognize that I _am_ as he sees me. Thus, shame can only be shame in the presence of an Other; I cannot be vulgar if I live on an island by myself. Moreover, shame does not reside _in_ the Other. I am responsible for it. The two structures are inseparable. Shame is (1) of oneself and (2) in the presence of an Other. At the same time, I need the Other in order to fully grasp all the structures of my being.

Like shame, pride and fear reveal to me the Other as a subject first, and only secondarily as an object. My original awareness of the Other is not one of judgment. It is rather an unmediated response to a foreign freedom. According to Sartre, fear is my awareness of my possibilities as these are transcended by the Other's freedom, and pride, my need of the Other to recognize my qualities and accomplishments as identified with me. Since without the Other I would have no objectivity, I need him to establish "my" qualities as intrinsically mine.

For me to be what I am, it suffices that the Other look at me. My "being seated" _is_ for the Other as this inkwell is on the table. My being caught on one knee, peering through a keyhole, is for the Other not a consciousness, not a free for-itself which is not what it is and is what it is not. Before the Other's look, I am ". . . leaning over the keyhole as this tree _is bent_ by the wind." (EN 321) Thus, it is shame that informs me that I am this particular being, in-itself. My _nature_ depends on the Other. My original fall, says Sartre, is the existence of the Other. My transcendence transcended is the Other's look.

This description, Sartre notes, has thus far been worked out on the level of the _cogito_. And yet, subjective reactions to the Other's look, e.g., fear, pride, and shame, those upon which the author has elaborated, are not provoked by a sudden irruption of knowledge. Rather, they point to a new stratification of the person which leaves intact his possibilities and structures "for-himself," but it places him suddenly in the new dimension of existence which Sartre calls the dimension of the <u>unrevealed</u>, i.e.,

> . . . an ecstatic [a Heideggerian term referring to the transcendent quality of time for human beings] relation of being, of which one term is the "I" as for-itself which is what it is not and is not what it is, and of which the other term is still the "I" but outside my reach, outside my action, outside my knowledge.(EN 327)

The latter term is connected with the infinite possibilities of an Other who is free, and therefore is "itself and infinite and inexhaustible synthesis of unrevealed properties." (EN 327)

The Other, then, cannot be an object for me. If he were, his being as-a-look would collapse. My attempts to objectify the Other are a maneuver on my part to preclude my being an object for him. But this will be taken up by Sartre, and by us, when the concrete relations with others are examined. For the present, and especially insofar as we are concerned with the phenomenon of the look, the Other is, by the foregoing description, that which no mere object can be. As Sartre explains,

> . . . He is the one who looks at me and at whom I am not yet looking, the one who delivers me to myself as <u>unrevealed</u>, but without revealing himself, the one who is present to me insofar as he "aims" at me but not as the object of my aim; he is the concrete and out-of-reach pole of my flight, of the alienation of my possibilities and of the flow of the world toward another world which <u>is the same</u> world and yet lacks all communication with this one. But he cannot be distinct from this very[17] alienation and flow; he is the meaning and the direction of them. . . . (EN 328)

As the Other looks at me, my world is transformed. Distances between myself and objects are denied, as they are now measured between objects and the Other. Ironically, the distance between me and various objects assumes significance for the Other. And as he constitutes me as standing at a certain distance from him, his presence to me is without distance. Thus, the "presence" is not reciprocal. Knowing this, Sartre says, enables us to explain the resistance which our common sense opposes to the solipsistic argument. I encounter the Other as a concrete presence. In no way can this presence have been derived from myself. Nor can it be revealed by any phenomenological reduction. When I am seen, I am aware of myself as an object-in-the-world, and of the Other-as-subject. This awareness, as Catalano notes, "has the character of an absolute experience, an irreducible fact that cannot be deduced from the objectivity of the world or from the nature of the for-itself."[18]

At the same time I experience the Other's subjectivity, I become aware of his infinite freedom. It is only for and through such a freedom that my own possibilities can be limited. As Sartre notes, a material object could not congeal my possibilities; it would simply be the necessary occasion for me to attempt other possibilities.

It is precisely for this reason that, according to Mary Warnock, Sartre claims that

> . . . such substances as treacle and honey are natural symbols of what we most hate in the world of things; they represent the "anti-value." For, instead of being tidy and manageable, such that we can pick them up, manipulate them and define their boundaries, they are glutinous and spreading, neither liquid nor solid, possessing us by their stickiness, which clings to our fingers if we try to shake it off.[19]

In regard to the Other, Warnock continues,

> But if the world of things sometimes oppresses us with its refusal to conform to our categories and obey our control, the world of people is far more distressing. Other people are themselves free, and can therefore, by numerous deliberate means, escape our attempts to predict or control them. . . . We tend to leave out of account the fact that they make plans and projects, frame intentions and form resolutions of their own. It is thus the _freedom_ of other people which is an outrage to us, and we try to overcome it by pretending it does not exist.[20]

There is a big difference between staying home because it is raining and staying home because one is forbidden to go out. The rain may deter me from venturing out, but only inasmuch as I may decide that I would rather stay in. In the case of someone else's forbidding me to go out, my possibilities both to stay in and to go out are presented to me as already fixed. "In the look," Sartre says, "the death of my possibilities makes me experience the freedom of the Other." (EN 330)

There is still another insight to be gained from the consideration of the Other's look. Suppose that as I crouched, peering through the keyhole, I thought I heard footsteps and was overtaken by a feeling of shame as I realized that someone must have seen me. Yet, as I search behind me, and up and down the corridor, and see no one there, I become aware that I was mistaken; it was a false alarm. Does that mean that the experience destroyed itself? Sartre asks. And he quickly answers, by no means!

Not only is the existence of the Other not placed in doubt, it has become even more certain after the false alarm. From the moment that I thought I heard footsteps, I become much more conscious of the possibility of being caught. Every little noise now suffices to make my heart beat faster. I am very much in a state of "being seen," even though there is no one there, at the moment, who is watching me. Nonetheless, I experience my being-for-the-Other as if he were there. What has been placed in doubt (through my awareness that I was mistaken when I thought there was someone there) is not the Other himself, but rather, Sartre notes, the <u>being-there</u> of the Other. We need, then, to examine the notion of the Other's <u>absence</u>, since it seems to be tied in with that of his presence.

It must be remembered that when we say that someone is absent from somewhere, it is always in reference to someone who could be expected to be present there. A student who has not signed up for my course cannot be considered absent on the first day of the semester, unless he had asked if he might sit in and was granted permission, in which case I should expect him to be present. Moreover, a person is absent always in reference to one or more persons. The place from which one is absent has significance only in relation to the Other, who expected him to be there. Thus, absence is really one of the ways of being present to someone else. Death is not absence, therefore. So long as I am alive, whether I am ten feet away from a person with whom I am in relation, or continents apart, I shall continue to be "present" to that person.

But it need not be the case that the relation between people "situates" one person or the other. As Sartre explains, I am a European in relation to the Asiatics, or an employer in relation to my workers. It is in relation to all living persons that human reality is present or absent against a background of original presence. And this original presence, the author contends, can have meaning only as "looking" or "being-looked-at": as a subject or as an object for another subject. To draw near, to move away, to leave, to stay, these are all ". . . empirical variations on the theme of being-for-the-Other." (EN 339)

Hartmann has criticized Sartre on this point for not being as thoroughgoing as he might have been. He contends that the French philosopher fails to

> . . . distinguish more carefully between the _direct_ encounter in the look and implicative phenomena like embarrassment, etc., which can be regarded as _indirect_ encounters with the Other. Bowing to the universality of our relationship to the Other, who is frequently absent, Sartre places greater emphasis on the indirect encounter.[21]

At first glance, this criticism appears to be valid. However, in light of the elaboration which follows, the more careful distinction which Hartmann desires would have backed Sartre into a corner from which he could emerge only by adopting Hegel's view of spirit as a dialectical unity, and this is something which Sartre wishes to avoid.

Besides, Sartre warns that although we can better understand the notion of the for-itself once we have grasped its relation to the Other, we must not assume that being-for-Others is an ontological structure of the for-itself. This supposition should be avoided, even though it would be difficult to conceive of a for-itself which was not simultaneously a for-another. Such a for-itself, according to Sartre, would simply not be a person. He avoids conjecturing about what such a for-itself would be, claiming that a work in phenomenological ontology need not concern itself with anthropology (EN 342). It is an empirical fact, revealed by the cogito, that our being, linked as it is with the for-itself, is linked at the same time with an Other. This is a claim which one would expect to read in Buber (and indeed such claims abound in his works), but it is surprising to find it proclaimed in _Being and Nothingness_, where the author has labored so diligently to disengage the for-itself from anything that _is_. As a matter of fact, the Other is not anything that is, rather it is a for-itself also, and therefore Sartre's contention in regard to this matter is consistent with his ontology.

There is another important observation to be made on this point. The for-itself, conscious of not being this or that, is conscious at the same time that it is different from that which is in-itself. There is no reciprocity in that case. However, in relation with an Other, I am conscious of not being he at the same time that he is conscious of not being I, and we are both aware, at the same time, that we are "beings" with similar "natures."

Why are there Others? We might as well ask why there is a for-itself, or why there is a world. Sartrean metaphysics invariably refers us to a fundamental contingency. The world and our consciousness do not have to be as they are--they just happen to be such. Ontology, Sartre says, explains the structure of the being of existents as a whole. Metaphysics puts into question the existence of the existent. As for the absolute contingency of the existent, "we are assured that all metaphysics must end with a 'that is how it is,' i.e., with a direct intuition of this contingency." (EN 359) But metaphysics, at this point, no matter how conceived, cannot elucidate Sartre's phenomenological ontology. We must turn now to the body, the manifestation of the Other's objectness for me, and mine for him, in order to grasp more fully the author's notion of Being-for-Others.

The Body

In alluding to the Other, whether to explain his look, my shame, or pride before him, his absence or his presence, Sartre has avoided specifying exactly how I view and relate to him. The for-itself is the nihilation of the in-itself. But is has not been articulated that the in-itself, as nihilated, is the body.

One of the problems in trying to understand the relation between body and consciousness is that we tend to link our consciousnesses with the bodies of others. As Sartre points out, when I describe a body it is never my own as it is *for me*. He says,

> I have never seen nor shall ever see my brain, nor my endocrine glands. But simply, from having seen men's cadavers dissected, I, who am a man, from what I have read in texts on physiology, conclude that my body is constituted exactly like all those whose color-plate representations I have seen in books. (EN 365)

Others may have seen my internal organs, but not I. The X-rays of my bones which I may have seen were objects in the world, like so many other objects. Only by a process of reasoning could I perceive them as *mine*. They are more accurately described as my *property* than as my *being*. When the doctor examines my injured leg and I sit up in my bed to see what he is doing, I perceive my own leg no differently from the way in which I see the body of the doctor (EN 365-66).

A distinction must be made between the body as a being for-itself and the body as a being-for-Others. Catalano notes that,

> Thus, while in the abstract our body is primarily a being-for-itself, in the concrete our body is also our alienated outwardness, and it is our consciousness as the concrete center of possibilities in the midst of a world of other centers of possibilities.[22]

Confusing the ontological planes of the abstract and the concrete results in absurdities such as the problem of "reversed vision" which physiologists used to pose, i.e., how do we reset upright the objects which are recorded upside down on the retina? Sartre notes that there is no problem in this for the philosopher. Things are right side up, or upside down, in reference to the rest of the universe. If we perceived the entire universe "upside down," we would consider what we perceived to be "rightside up." The point which Sartre really wants to make is that this problem illustrates the common error of trying to tie _my_ awareness of objects with the body of _others_. By creating a model of a candle, a lens which represents the lens in _my eye_, and an upside-down candle on a screen which represents _my retina_, the physiologist confuses my body as for-itself with my body as for-others. The eye depicted in the model, like the eye which I see in the mirror, is the eye which the Other sees when he looks at me. The two planes of Being are not reducible, the one to the other. The for-itself is wholly body and wholly consciousness, according to Sartre. It would not make sense to say that it is connected to a body. Similarly, being-for-others is entirely body; there are no psychic phenomena to be joined to it (EN 368). Sartre's elaboration of these two modes of "being one's body" comprises the major part of his chapter on _the body_.

Facticity

As noted above,[23] a man's facticity is contingent in two respects. Not being the foundation of its own being, it is contingent that his consciousness exists. On the other hand, it is fortuitous that a man is "thrown" (as Heidegger puts it) into the world with a particular genetic and social background, in a particular geographical area, at a particular time in the evolution and history of mankind. Consciousness is perpetually aware of its contingency. It is haunted by it, and it is thus constantly reminded that it is unjustifiable, yet totally responsible for itself.

The body is the point of reference and origin of meaning of the world as a system of relations. For _me_, the telephone is to the left of the dictionary. For my students, it is to the right. For every for-itself, the world is uniquely ordered. There is no one, hovering above the world, for whom the phone is at the same time both to the right and to the left. This is what Sartre means when he says that the order of the world is also the facticity of the for-itself--for it is _my_ for-itself which makes this particular order of the world exist and yet which escapes me since I am not the foundation of my being. In this sense, Sartre says, the body could be defined as ". . . the contingent form which the necessity of my contingency takes." (EN 371)

To explain how the world comes-to-be through the for-itself, Sartre provides an analysis of that form of knowledge which is obtained from the senses. He rejects the realist theory because, he says, it is contradictory. The realist dissects, examines, experiments, and draws conclusions about the eyes, ears, etc., by focusing his own organs on those of the Other. Thus, it is the Other's eyes which are the source of information on perception, not his own, and then the data derived, which are clearly subjective, are offered as objective. How do we know for sure that our observations about the Other's sense organs made with our own sense organs, are valid, Sartre asks.

The whole notion of sensation, we are told, is absurd (EN 377). It is pure invention. It does not correspond to anything used in our experiments on ourselves or the Other. All that we have ever been able to grasp has been the objective world. All our determinations (negations) assume that there is a world, and come-to-be in relation to it. Theories of sensation, however, take for granted that a man, since he is equipped with sensory organs, is already _in_ the world. Ironically, the sensations are seen as breaks in a man's relations with the world, and these transcendent relations, which were made to disappear by the sensations, are supposed to be reestablished upon a new ground, which realists call pure subjectivity. Sartre regards this explanation as circular: my perception of the Other's sense organs provides for me the basis for any explanation of sensations in general and of my own sensations in particular. On the other hand, my sensations, thus conceived, constitute the only _reality_ of my perception of the Other's senses (EN 378).

In contrast with the realist's account, Sartre claims that sensation is an aspect of the event whereby the for-itself surges into the world by negating the in-itself. As it does so, the for-itself is not identified with this shape, that color, that sound, etc. But every negation results in a determination, and so the negations through which the for-itself emerges as not-color, not-sound, etc., at the same time bring about the determinations of colors, sounds, etc. Our senses do not come before the objects, nor do they come after. They are contemporaneous with them. "They are even," according to Sartre,

> . . . the objects in person, such as they unveil themselves to us in perspective. They simply represent an objective rule of this unveiling. Thus, sight does not _produce_ visual sensations; nor is it _affected_ by rays of light, but rather it is the collection of all the visible objects inasmuch as their objective and reciprocal relations all refer to certain chosen sizes. . . . Thus, it is the surging of the for-itself into the world which brings about with one stroke the existence of the world as the totality of things and the senses as the objective manner in which the qualities of things present themselves. (EN 382-83)

Gilbert Ryle seems to express a similar insight when he explains the logic of sensation and observation. He says,

> It is true that the cobbler cannot witness the tweaks that I feel when the shoe pinches. But it is false that I witness them. The

reason why my tweaks cannot be witnessed by him is not that some Iron Curtain prevents them from being witnessed by anyone save myself, but that they are not the sorts of things of which it makes sense to say that they are witnessed or unwitnessed at all, even by me. I feel or have the tweaks, but I do not discover or peer at them; they are not things that I find out about by watching them, listening to them, or savoring them. In the sense in which a person may be said to have had a robin under observation, it would be nonsense to say that he has had a twinge under observation. There may be one or several witnesses of a road accident; there cannot be several witnesses, or even one witness, of a qualm.[24]

The body, says Sartre, is not only the "seat of the five senses," but also, "The instrument and the goal of our actions." (EN 383) Actions and sensations are indistinguishable if we apply the classical psychological meaning to these terms, and therefore, the analysis of the senses can serve as a guide to the study of the body. Just as we must guard against explicating my sensation by observing the Other's, so too must we be careful not to interpret my actions by observing the various components of someone else's actions. Since the Other's are the only ones which I can see "unfolding," the risk is great to assume that my own actions are performed in the identical manner.

The Other's body appears to me not only as an instrument which can make tools, but one which operates tools as well. If I were to construe the role which my body plays in respect to my actions from basing my conclusions on what I know about the Other's body, I would consider myself able to dispose of an instrument which can create and manipulate tools according to the ends which I wish to achieve, and that account, we are reminded, would lead us back to the classical distinction of the soul and the body, and the concomitant problem of how to explain their interaction (EN 384). It would also parallel the fallacy of taking as granted that I can know about my senses by observing those of the Other.

It is only rarely that we consider our body as an instrument. In Sartre's view, our body is the center of reference as the for-itself surges into the world, from which and toward which the world is ordered. Marjorie Grene points out that,

> His [Sartre's] argument leads him to the insight that our sense-mediated interaction with the world, is necessarily tied to its point of origin, the point of view that is my bodily being.[25]

If I rearrange the furniture in my room, certain surfaces will no longer be usable or even visible to me, whereas other surfaces will become visible and usable. There is no mind, however, which can know all the surfaces of things from an absolute vantage point. In Catalano's interpretation, if there were some absolute viewpoint,

> . . . their [the uses and surfaces of things] very reality as relations in the world would vanish. On the contrary, they must be ordered to something that is both the origin of their relations and that retains their reality as relations in the world. It is to the human reality as a body that the instrumentality, the place, and the perspective of things are ordered; and it is because the human reality is a body that these relations are transcendencies in the world and not merely ideas in the mind.[26]

As the for-itself surges into being, the world reveals itself as an indication of actions to be performed, and these point to further actions that are possible, etc. Although perception and action are indistinguishable, they are different in that actions aim at or point to the future, whereas that which is perceived comes-to-be simultaneously with the for-itself. As such, the perceived cannot be seized. It is the pure "being there" of things, Sartre contends. It <u>belongs</u> to the for-itself, it is its facticity, its body. Our body is our immediate past. We flee from it toward our possibilities. It is in this sense that our body is our finitude, the center of reference of our world. When perception "runs ahead" toward action, the world is revealed as a "hollow which is always future," (EN 386) because the for-itself is always future to itself.

Sartre's analysis of the "usability" or instrumentality of things in the world is thorough and complex. It takes into account the notions of intentionality in Husserl, of transcendence in Heidegger, and it touches on the theory of the "coefficient of adversity" of objects which Bachelard had introduced. We need not be detained here by an exhaustive account of Sartre's phenomenological version. Perhaps the most important idea to be gleaned from it is that usability precedes intentionality in that objects reveal themselves as instruments and, as these come into the world simultaneously with the for-itself, they are not "intended" until after our body is indicated as their center of reference. Thus we "live" our body. As Sartre says,

> Our body extends at all times through the instrument which it employs; it is at the end of the stick on which I lean, against the ground; at the end of the telescope which enables me to see the stars; on the chair; in the entire house because it is my adaptation to these instruments. (EN 389)

The point which Sartre wants to emphasize is that his explanation avoids the common error of positing a person's body first and then proceeding to examine the manner in which the person grasps the world, or modifies it, through his body. It is more accurate to describe the process, according to Sartre, as one in which the instruments, as they originally appear in the world make me aware of my body. "In one sense," he says, "the body is what I am immediately; in another sense I am separated from it by the infinite density of the world. . . ." (EN 390)

In his explanation of the nature-for-us of our body, Sartre provides a clear account of the "necessity of our contingency" of which our body is the contingent form. The body, as noted, is our facticity. It is that which we have been. At the same time, it is that which we are to be. We are perpetually a choice, but we perpetually choose ourselves anew. The body is the necessity that there be a choice. We never grasp the contingency of our body prereflectively. If we are born with an infirmity, or become handicapped by accident, we live our lives "through" our infirmity. We may choose it as an obstacle, or as a challenge. It may be a source of shame or of pride. We cannot choose ourselves "all at once," anyway. It is contingent that we are Caucasian or Black, poor or rich, short or tall. We exist our body through these conditions. Our body is our prereflective cogito which shapes the world at the same time that it is shaped by it. More often than not, it is the Other who makes us aware of being "what we are," i.e., rich or poor, normal or handicapped, etc.

Indeed, we can be conscious of our body. We need but reflect on how" it feels." If we are in pain, it is often the case that the pain has been present for some time before we become aware of it. We may succeed in surpassing the discomfort (e.g., by ignoring it, distracting ourselves, etc.) but we do so only temporarily, for it "returns" as we become aware once again that it hurts. As for the exact location of the pain, that too, is something or somewhere which consciousness "exists." Most of the time, our eyes serve us in reading printed material, for example, without our being in any way conscious of our eyes. It is the words, sentences, etc., on which we concentrate, and even these are but signs or symbols, frequently, or abstract thoughts and relations of our intentionality. The Other may notice our eyes, but we do not--unless we stop to reflect about them. If they hurt, if we have difficulty, we are forced to take notice of our eyes. At this point it is not a pain-in-the-eyes. It is difficulty of reading, blurred print, need to reread, etc. Only after reflection do we fix precisely what and where it is.[27]

Physical pain is a convenient example of "existing one's contingency." Many other examples could be cited, although some lend themselves to a clearer phenomenological examination than others. Sartre claims that even when consciousness is not drawn to any particular comfort or discomfort of the body, it projects itself beyond its contingency. It continues to exist its body, vaguely grasping itself as bland, colorless, without distance, yet clinging. The for-itself grasps it as its "taste" a taste which Sartre has described as *nausea*, and on which he has elaborated extensively.[28]

The Body for Others

By now, Sartre has made clear that in his ontology, my body appears in exactly the same fashion to the Other as his body appears to me. Therefore, he elects to study the ontological dimension of the body-for-others from the perspective of the Other's body-for-me, as this approach is more convenient. It is important to remember that the Other does not manifest himself initially through his body. If such were the case, the relation between us would be one of externality, and that, we have noted, would create insuperable problems. It is rather because I am conscious of being seen, because of the look and its implications that the existence of the Other is revealed to me. We must study the relation, then, as one in which, first, the Other exists for me and I for him, and in which his body and mine, as ontological structures, figure secondarily.

This secondary role assigned to the body of the Other must not be construed as implying that his body is perceived and understood as an instrument among other instruments (unless, Sartre points out, we are speaking of the Other's cadaver). There is something unique about the object which is the Other's body. As Catalano notes,

> Just as my own body is the necessary way in which I exist my contingency, the other's body-for-me is a revelation of the necessity of his contingency, the manifestation of the facticity of his transcendence, and the synthetic relation of the other as a body-in-a-situation.[29]

I can transcend the Other's body as a point of view, but still there will be objects which retain a "secondary and oblique order of reference to him."[30] Indeed, it is the pattern of objects in relation to other bodies which indicates my own body to me. I can never seize the Other's body without seizing at the same time my own as the center of reference to which the Other points. The Other's body is thus "significant" (in the sense that it "signals") since it indicates the relations between bodies and objects.

The Other's body is a synthetic totality for me. I cannot apprehend his body unless it be within the context of a total situation. Nor can I perceive in isolation a particular organ of the Other's body; I see it always within the context of his life, his activity, or his flesh. Thus, I do not notice an arm rising alongside an immobile body, but rather I see that _Peter is raising his arm_. A photograph may "magnify" the size of Peter's hand if he holds it in front of the camera as the picture is being snapped, but with the naked eye, such distortion will not take place, for I see him in a situation which Sartre has called the "synthetic totality of life and action." (EN 413)

One might ask, along with Grene,

> . . . what has happened to the Other as Consciousness? Other as body, Sartre has insisted, is posterior to that first, hemmorrhagic starting into being of the Other which threatens to organize the world around him and so drains me away from myself.[31]

There are other difficulties with Sartre's position on this matter. Both Grene and Merleau-Ponty[32] have argued that Sartre's treatment of language (as a form of seduction) leaves untapped the concepts of human community and of psychophysical unity, among others.

A person's character, in Sartre's account, is the same as his facticity. Since the other is free to transcend his contingency, his body is always "past" in a manner which he has chosen. His character, then, is his facticity insofar as it is accessible to my intuition. I see a pattern of his past and present behavior, I intuit the possibilities of his behaving differently, and I am aware of his freedom to transcend the pattern. The totality of this intuition is what I consider the Other's character to be.

The Third Ontological Dimension of the Body

The first dimension of the being of the body is facticity. I exist my body as its immediate past. The second dimension is the body-for-others. The Other knows and uses my body, just as I know an use his. In the third dimension, Sartre notes, I exist for myself as known by the Other (who reveals himself as the subject for whom I am an object) and therefore I exist my body as a transcendence transcended.

Being there, Sartre says, is precisely the body. I cannot quite know or conceive my "self" as in-itself for the Other, yet I am aware of its flight toward another being who is in the midst of the world. Thus, although primarily consciousness is for-itself, in the presence of the Other an essential modification takes place. I become aware of an "outer" aspect of my "inner" reality. To say that one feels himself blushing or perspiring is to express improperly the fact that one is aware of his body such as it is not for himself, but for an Other.[33]

It would seem, at first, that only my consciousness is modified by the look of the Other, and that my body, as I exist it and as it is known by the Other, remains unaffected. But since my body is the facticity of my consciousness, the Other's look radically affects the way in which I exist my body.

The "outer" aspect of my body can be grasped prereflectively, i.e., I am conscious that this body which the Other sees and perhaps judges is not a mere object in the world, it is *mine*. Moreover, I am alienated from it since it is my exterior which is seen and judged by numerous Others, whose freedoms escape me. But I have access to my body reflectively also. I can learn to know my body as it is for the Other through language. The process is uncomplicated. At first, I learn to know the Other's body through language. Thereafter, I apply the same concepts to my own. As Catalano explains,

> Before this, my alienation from my body was lived without any concepts intervening. Then, as we learn to know the other's senses as organs for knowing and his body as an instrument of his consciousness, we likewise learn to understand our senses and our body in this manner.[34]

At this point, Sartre notes, we are ready to pursue our analysis of "pain" in greater depth than before. We are reminded that a "stomach ache" is really the stomach itself as "it is lived painfully." When we reflect on the duration and intensity of the pains, we may conclude that they are caused by illness, and we comprehend disorders and diseases as concepts which we have learned from our knowledge of the Other (or which he has learned from us). The disease exists for the Others even when I am not afflicted by it. It is they who can explain it, diagnose it. The doctor becomes responsible for my illness. When I avoid drinking wine, if I suffer from hepatic colic, I do so in order not to reawaken the pains in my liver. "But my precise aim," Sartre explains, "not to reawaken the pains in my liver, cannot be distinguished in any way from this other aim: to obey the prohibitions of my doctor who revealed them to me." (EN 425)

The fact that we can see our body, touch it, etc., is purely contingent. It is certainly not an indication of how we acquire knowledge about it. According to Sartre, it is a "curiosity" of our constitution that in certain well defined cases, our body can appear to us like that of an Other. This particularity could not be deduced from the necessity that the for-itself have a body, nor from the structures of the body-for-another.

We are so constituted that one hand can touch the other. Our eyes can perceive many parts of our body but not all. One eye cannot see the other, nor can one see the back of one's head. It must be noted, however, that these perceptions do not reveal the body as acting and grasping, but rather as acted upon and grasped. Nor is there anything surprising about this phenomenon, in Sartre's account. If one acknowledges surprise at any of these claims, it is evidence, according to the author, that one "has seized the necessity of the for-itself to surge into the world as a concrete point of view. . . ." (EN 427)

Concrete Relations with the Other

As noted at the start of this chapter, Sartre's paramount concern has never been the Other. By far the most important notion in *Being and Nothingness* is the for-itself. The Other, the in-itself, facticity, these and many other notions serve as lenses through which we can focus more clearly on the human reality which Sartre equates with the individual's consciousness. Nevertheless, he recognizes a certain reciprocity at play in intersubjective relations, and almost reluctantly concedes that the Other affects not only my consciousness, but indeed, the way in which I exist my body as well. In this section, Sartre describes concrete relations with the Other. Again, these are conveniently broken down so as to fit neatly into categories that follow the author's scheme.

Our relations with Others can be classified in one of two ways: (1) we can confer objectivity on the Other so as to retain our own subjectivity, or (2) we can assimilate the Other's freedom into our own while at the same time trying to preserve his freedom. If we could succeed in obtaining the Other's *free* recognition of our own subjectivity, we would thereby become our own foundation (EN 430), but the fact is that we cannot succeed in this project any more than we can confer objectivity on the Other in order to retain our subjectivity. Since each project implies the other, they are both impossible to achieve. The failure of one attitude motivates the adoption of the other, so that our relations with Others are not dialectical, but rather circular, and we cannot break out of the circle. Simply stated, in our effort to preserve the Other's freedom, we transform it into an object, since it is *we* who are endeavoring to preserve it. On the other hand, if we objectify the Other in order to preserve our freedom we recognize the freedom of a subject in the ostensibly objectified Other.

It is worthwhile quoting Sartre directly on the theme of being-for-others, as his words exemplify better than any others his opinion about interpersonal relations:

> Everything that goes for me goes for the Other. While I try to free myself from the grasp of the Other, he tries to free himself from mine; while I try to enslave the Other, he tries to enslave me. It is not at all a questions of unilateral relations with an object-in-itself, but of reciprocal and dynamic relations. The descriptions which follow must therefore be viewed in the perspective of conflict. <u>Conflict is the original sense of being-for-others</u>. (EN 431, emphasis mine)

There are, then, two attitudes toward the Other. One attitude is exemplified by love, language and masochism, and the other attitude, by indifference, desire, hate, and sadism. As Sartre explains the difference between the two attitudes, it becomes clear what the elements in each of these two lists have in common. Neither takes precedence in time, importance, inclination, etc. Therefore, we could begin with the examination of either one, and we shall start arbitrarily with the first.

In love, language, masochism, I respect the subjectivity of the Other in order to obtain recognition for my own. However, I can preserve the Other's subjectivity only be remaining an object for him. As Salvan has explained it,

> The other, in a sense, <u>possesses</u> my being as I shall never possess it. He gives me form, color, concreteness; and he does so freely, simply by seeing me as I am. This concrete existence which the other confers on me, is the indication of what I should like to ground in liberty so as to be my own foundation. . . . (But in order to preserve

the other's subjectivity, I must first of all remain an object for him...,[35]

The aim of love is to be loved. Therefore, the ideal of love is doomed to failure. Both the one who loves and the one who is loved attempt to become the object of fascination, both attempt to beguile and seduce the Other's freedom and subjectivity. The only reason that the project of love continues is that the one who loves does not realize, or else, in bad faith, chooses not to realize, that the one who is loved is engaged in the same project.

Language also, according to Sartre, is a form of seduction of the Other's freedom. It is through language that I strive to regain my alienated self, by adopting the Other's viewpoint concerning myself. I objectify myself in order to establish contact as in-itself for the Other and thereafter I attempt to change his view to my advantage. Quoting Heidegger's phrase, "I am what I say," Sartre goes on to describe language as,

> ... part of the **human condition**, it is originally the test that a for-itself can make of its in-itself, and ultimately going beyond that test and using it for possibilities which are my possibilities, i.e., for possibilities of my being this and that for the Other. (EN 441)

Sartre does not limit his interpretation of language to the spoken word, but rather includes any form of expression all. As a matter of fact, he considers the articulate word a secondary, derivative mode of expressive phenomenon. It should be noted that language is not always a form of seduction. We are fascinated by an orator, an actor, a juggler, but that does not mean that we love him. Nevertheless, language as well as other forms of expression are an appeal to the Other's subjectivity, to his transcendence.

Masochism is described as an attempt (also doomed to failure) to remain an object for the Other permanently. If this could be achieved, the for-itself would have surrendered to the Other the task of making it exist. It would become in-itself and thereby forgo its subjectivity. But the masochist crawls on his knees in vain, Sartre indicates; he deludes himself only briefly by assuming a demeaning posture, or letting himself be used as a simple, inanimate object. The fact is that it is for the Other that he is obscene or passive. For himself he is condemned forever to being the one who chooses to exist masochistically!

The second attitude toward the Other, it may be recalled, is exemplified in indifference, desire, hate, and sadism. Having met with failure upon adoption of the first attitude, a person may turn to the second. Or else, one could have failed with the second, in which case he would now resort to the first.

Since we are unable to appropriate the Other's freedom within our own, we may attempt to confront his freedom directly. Admittedly, this attempt is equally futile, since in order to succeed we would have to look at the Other while he was looking at us, and in so doing we would be objectifying his look, thus creating, as it were, a looked-at look. We would be seeing his eyes, but not his look.

In the stance of indifference, I avoid confronting the Other's freedom altogether. I treat him as an object, ignoring completely the fact of his subjectivity. Catalano names this project "practical solipsism." Salvan labels it "voluntary solipsism." Sartre describes it as **factual solipsism**, whereby I use people as means toward my own ends. I overlook, in bad faith, the fact that the other people's absolute subjectivity is the foundation of my being-in-itself and being-for-others. Their objectified freedom becomes for me but their "coefficient of adversity." Sounding almost like Buber, Sartre declares that a man can pursue this attitude for along time--for years--for a whole lifetime. "There are men," he says, "who die without ever having realized, except for brief and terrifying flashes, what the Other is all about." (EN 449) What do these flashes reveal to such men? Perhaps the fact that although they have made the Other's look into a pair of eyes, they are aware, especially in moments of anxiety, that the Other _sees_ them, and the more they try to objectify the Other, the more they jeopardize their tenuous state of indifference toward him.

Sexual desire is consiousness of desire. It is not necessarily the case that man is a sexual being because he has a sex. Sartre claims that it is the other way around. Children are sexual, as are eunuchs and old people. The physiological state of one's sexual organ can no more account for sexual desire than the dilation of one's pupils can explain or provoke fear. In Sartre's terms, to be sexual means, given the description of the body in the preceding section,

> . . .to exist sexually for an Other who exists sexually for me. . . . Considered from the point of view of the for-itself, this realization of the sexuality of the Other cannot be in the pure, disinterested contemplation of his primary or secondary sexual characteristics. . . . The first apprehension of the sexuality of the Other, inasmuch as it is lived and suffered, cannot be anything but _desire; it is in desiring the Other_ (or in discovering myself incapable of desiring him) _or in grasping his desire of me, that I discover his sexual being_; and desire reveals to me simultaneously _my_ sexual being and _his, my_ body as sex and _his_ body. (EN 453 emphasis mine)

Several more fallacies need to be dispelled. Sexual desire is not the desire to "possess" the Other in the sense that possessing might mean "making love to."

Nor is sexual desire the desire "for a woman," but rather, the woman is the end of the desire. Only the thought that the sexual act suppresses desire can account for the opinion which fails to distinguish between desire of sexual desire and sexual desire of the Other. Desire is not desire of any particular sexual act, as evidence by the fact that there are so many of these. Desire, generally speaking, is not the desire *to do* anything. It is simply and purely desire of a <u>transcendent being</u>.

By desire, we attempt to make the Other limit himself freely to his body and thus become identified with his facticity and objectivity. We want to possess his body exactly as it is possessed by his freedom. At the same time, we choose ourselves in the same way. We make ourselves flesh in order to bring about the incarnation of the Other. We shall return to Sartre's account of sexual desire when we compare it to the explanation put forward by Buber.

In sadism also, one tries to incarnate the Other's consciousness, to make him aware of his body through pain and suffering, and thereby force him to recognize his objectivity. Catalano summarizes clearly the descriptions offered by Sartre:

> The sadist aims at the obscene in order to strip the body of its grace, reducing it to a thing to capture within this thing the other's freedom. Unlike desire, in which freedom envelops and incarnates the body as flesh, sadism aims at revealing flesh as capturing and containing freedom. The use of torture and pain to bring the other to renounce all that he cherishes reduces the body to a flesh that is this very enslaved freedom.[36]

As with all attitudes toward the Other, sadism carries the seeds of its own destruction. As the sadist, by means of torture, is about to achieve his aim, i.e., force his victim to yield, to renounce his freedom, he finds that he is now confronting a mere object of flesh. At this point, he may desire it sexually, or he may be "troubled" by this absurd spectacle. More significantly, the sadist glimpses his failure in the look of the victim, wherein the latter reaffirms his transcendent freedom and the former apprehends himself as an object, an instrument inflicting pain, in the victim's world.[37]

In hatred, the individual wants to do away with others as transcendence, but usually focuses on a single person, or a group, as objects of hate. The person who truly hates is not disturbed by this or that particular trait in the Other; it is the Other's existence which bothers him. Of course, to do away with his transcendence, he must first recognize it as such, and therefore hatred also fails to achieve its aim. If one could succeed in suppressing others, he would thereby become the living memory of their existence. They would thenceforth be part of him, a part which he could never change or destroy.

The fundamental attitudes toward the Other outlined above are not meant to encompass all of the possible postures one can assume, and they certainly do not exhaust all the issues regarding sexuality. But, according to Sartre, sexuality is a primitive attitude toward the Other which necessarily encompasses the original contingency of being-for-others as well as of the being-for-itself. Given a situation in which there is a body and an Other, there is at the same time a reaction of desire, love, and the derived attitudes described above. "Our physiological make-up," Sartre contends, "merely reflects symbolically and on the ground of absolute contingency the permanent possibility that we are to assume one or the other of the attitudes." (EN 477)

The reason for Sartre's minute examination of the question of sexuality is twofold. First, as we have noted, he considers it fundamental in interpersonal relations. Second, he believes that all the other complex forms of behavior among people are but elaborations of the two original ones. Thus, the concrete forms of behavior themselves, e.g., collaboration, struggle, rivalry, emulation, pity, are much more difficult to analyze, as these depend on the historical situation and the concrete particularity of each relation between a self and an Other.

Being-With (Mitsein) and the "We"

Sartre's chief criticism of Heidegger's notion of being-with is not that we never experience the "we". Indeed we do experience it, and Sartre provides a clear description of its many manifestations. What he denies, however, is that being-with is the foundation of our relation with the Other, or even that it constitutes an ontological structure of human reality. He denies that it is intersubjective, that it is greater than the sum of its parts, that it is some sort of collective consciousness, as some sociologists have claimed. Decidedly, Sartre says, being-for-others precedes and is the foundation of being-with-others.

Language often provides clues as to the manner in which we view the world and our role in it. It has been argued that much of what we think is colored by the syntactic and semantic structures of the language in which we think.[38] Sartre seems to agree, when he declares that "perhaps we should revise completely the question and study the relation of language to thought in a completely new form." (EN 484) The fact that in most languages there are different forms for _we_ (as subject) and for _us_ (as object)[39] is an indication that we experience ourselves as a plurality of subjects, i.e., as transcending-transcendences and not as transcended-transcendences when we use the nominative form. On the other hand, the form employed in sentences such as "They can see me" clearly indicates that I experience myself as an object, as myself alienated, as a transcendence-transcended. The two forms, then, correspond to the paradigmatic being-who-is-looking and being-who-is-looked at.

The accusative case 'us', refers to the experience of a single individual who is aware that he is part of a group of human beings who are objectified together. The background of my relations with the Other is the __detotalized-totality__, Sartre's characterization of humanity (in the sense that a consciousness which is divorced from the totality can never really witness it and form it into a synthetic whole). The prototype of this background is the "third" who may come upon the scene as I interact with the Other. Whatever my attitude toward the Other may be at that moment, and his toward me, I become aware of that attitude as it is objectified by the "third." My totality and the Other's are temporarily joined as the outsider objectifies us together.

The concrete existence of a "third" is not essential to the us-relation. The for-itself is pre-reflectively aware that many Others coexist with it, and that therefore it can be temporarily joined with one or more Others by one or more "thirds." The for-itself is aware also that it can be joined with the totality of human beings (as in "suffering humanity" or "sinful humanity") in the eyes of an absolute "third," who is distinct from humanity and in whose eyes the whole of humanity is an object. This is the concept of God, as Sartre views it. God is he for whom man can never be a "third." He is the "looking" being who can never be "looked at." This description is similar to Buber's with respect to the Eternal Thou who can never be addressed as "it."

Since Sartre construes all relations between human beings as conflict situations, it is understandable that 'us' takes on a meaning which is not typical in language, nor in thought. Siblings who express contentment as they assert "our parents will protect us," statesmen who are proud to announce to their countrymen that the Nobel Committee "is honoring us," and countless other examples which could be given, contradict Sartre's contention that the use of 'us' necessarily implies a humiliating experience. When he says that "the oppressed class finds its class unity in the cognizance which the oppressing class takes of it, and the appearance in the appressed of class-consciousness corresponds to the assumption, in shame, of an 'us'," (EN 493) one is led to suspect that the author may be stretching the point.

Footnotes

1. About Sartre's prose, Natanson writes, "It is impossible to convey to anyone who has not read l'Etre et le néant the involved and often tangled line of Sartre's argument and the horrifying quality of the prose which is intended to convey the author's ideas." *A Critique of Jean-Paul Sartre's Ontology* (Lincoln, Neb.: University of Nebraska Studies, March 1951), p. 19.

2. Maurice Merleau-Ponty, *Phénoménologie de la perception* (Paris: Editions Gallimard, 1945), p. 369. (Translation mine.)

3. Gilbert Varet, *L'Ontologie de Sartre* (Paris: Presses Universitaires de France, 1948), p. 104. (Translation mine.)

4. In *Les Mouches*, Orestes wishes that he were not burdened with his freedom and several times considers giving into the temptation of abrogating it. In contrast, in *Huis Clos*, Garcin would like to disassociate himself from his past actions which, he says, cling to him like a ball and chain. In both plays, the protagonists come to realize that their wishes are but fantasies which can never be fulfilled.

5. The subtitle of *Being and Nothingness* is *An Essay in Phenomenological Ontology*.

6. Of these, Jacques Salvan's *To Be or Not to Be: An Analysis of Jean Paul Sartre's Ontology*, is perhaps the best known in America. Joseph Catalano's *A Commentary on Jean-Paul Sartre's "Being and Nothingness"* (New York: Harper Torchbooks, 1974), is perhaps the most comprehensive. An even more complete summary can be obtained by referring to the numerous essays which have been published in journals, collections of essays, etc., regarding particular aspects of Sartre's philosophy.

7. George L. Kline, "The Existentialist Rediscovery of Hegel and Marx," in *Sartre*, ed. Mary Warnock (Garden City, N.Y.: Doubleday & Col, 1971), p. 284-314.

8. Ibid., p. 285.

9. Klaus Hartmann, *Sartre's Ontology: A Study of Being and Nothingness in the Light of Hegel's Logic* (Evanston: Northwestern University Press, 1966), pp. 284-314.

10. Marjorie Grene has given a clear account of the types of influence Hegel exerted on Sartre. She says: "And what Sartre takes over from Hegel is not the empirical content of his work, though sometimes he treats of some of it, nor his insight into history; what Sartre adopts from Hegel goes much deeper than any particular bits of information or ways of classifying them. Admittedly, the Hegelian influence comes relatively late in Sartre's career, but it goes deep. Sartre is Hegelian, and has become increasingly so, first in his style of philosophizing, in the way he uses concepts. Further, the central concepts he uses, both in *Being and Nothingness* and in the *Critique*, also belong, if not to Hegel, then certainly to the German tradition. And finally, however emphatically he may claim to reject systematizing speculation in general, and idealist systems in particular, there is also something in Hegel's ontology itself that Sartre retains" (*Sartre*, p. 79).

11. See pp. 18-20 above.

12. See p. 15 above.

13. Jean-Paul Sartre, *Huis Clos, suivi de Les Mouches* (Paris: Editions Gallimard, 1947), p. 75.

14. In her translation of EN, (=BN 250) Hazel Barnes mistakenly, translates *croître* and *décroître* as 'believe' and 'disbelieve.' It is probable that she confused the French *croire* [to believe] with *croître* [to 'increase', 'to grow']. However, *décroître* ['to decrease'] has no such homonym as *décroire* and therefore we must assume that Ms. Barnes took it to mean the opposite of *croire*.

15. One of the conditions which Sartre has proposed above has thus been met.

16. Catalano, A <u>Commentary</u>, pp. 162-63.

17. Hazel Barnes translates, *cette alienation même* as 'this same alienation,' (BN 269) overlooking the fact that commonly, in French, when *même* follows the noun it modifies, it means 'itself' or 'very'.

18. Catalano, A <u>Commentary</u>, p. 166.

19. Warnock, <u>Existentialist Ethics</u>, pp. 44-45.

20. Ibid., p. 45.

21. Hartmann, <u>Sartre's Ontology</u>, p. 113.

22. Catalano, A <u>Commentary</u>, p. 169.

23. See p. 38 above.

24. Ryle, <u>Concept of Mind</u>, p. 205.

25. Grene, <u>Sartre</u>, p. 166.

26. Catalano, A <u>Commentary</u>, p. 173.

27. Sartre finds in this alternation of being conscious of pain, "fleeing" it, and becoming conscious of it again an analogy with the reciprocal relation of the for-itself negating the in-itself (surpassing it), and the in-itself, as facticity, reappropriating the for-itself. (EN, p. 399).

28. See *La Nausée* and *La Mort dans l'âme*. In both of these novels Sartre describes meticulously the feelings of nausea which frequently overtake the protagonists.

29. Catalano, *A Commentary*, p. 176.

30. Ibid.

31. Grene, *Sartre*, p. 170.

32. Merleau-Ponty, *Phénoménologie de la perception*, Pt. I, ch. 6.

33. A good illustration of this phenomenon can be found in T. S. Eliot's poem, "The Love Song of J. Alfred Prufrock."

34. Catalano, *A Commentary*, p. 179.

35. Jacques Salvan, *To Be and Not To Be* (Detroit: Wayne State University Press, 1962), p. 87.

36. Catalano, *A Commentary*, p. 187.

37. Sartre illustrates movingly this particular phenomenon by quoting, from a French translation of William Faulkner's *Light in August*, (New York: Random House, 1932), p. 407, a passage in which a Black has just been emasculated,

"But the man on the floor had not moved. He just lay there, with his eyes open and empty of everything save consciousness, and with something, a shadow, about his mouth. For a long moment he looked up at them with peaceful and unfathomable and unbearable eyes. Then his face, body, all, seemed to collapse, to fall in upon itself, and from out the slashed garments about his hips and loins the pent black blood seemed to rush like a released breath. It seemed to rush out of his pale body like the rush of sparks from a rising rocket; upon that black blast the man seemed to rise soaring into their memories forever and ever. They are not to lose it, in whatever peaceful valleys, beside whatever placid and reassuring streams of old age, in the mirroring faces of whatever children they will contemplate old disasters and newer hopes. It will be there, musing, quiet, steadfast, not fading and not particularly threatful, but of itself alone serene, of itself alone triumphant." (En 476)

38. Cf. Alfred North Whitehead's *Symbolism: Its Meaning and Effect* [1927] (New York: Capricorn Books, G. P. Putnam's Sons, 1959); and Jerrold J. Katz's *The Underlying Reality of Language and its Philosophical Import* (New York: Harper Torchbooks, Harper & Row, 1971).

39. French uses the same form, *nous*, but its syntax provides for numerous distinctions between the nominative and accusative cases.

CHAPTER III

OBSERVATIONS ON SARTRE'S POINT OF VIEW

As noted in the Introduction, an effort was made to keep the (preceding) section on Sartre's ontology free from critical comments which, however appropriate, would have interrupted the continuity of the exposition. The author has been allowed to state his argument, as it were, without reactions from the audience. Clearly, much has been lost in the interpretation. Oversimplification necessarily results in distortion. Selection of points which needed elaboration and those which could be omitted for the sake of brevity was not easy. However, it was felt that since works like *Being and Nothingness* are rarely read from beginning to end more than once by even the most dedicated scholars, the synopsis of applicable sections, if done intelligently, would serve a useful purpose.

At this point it will be profitable to consider some of the comments which have been made in favor of and against Sartre's account. Emotional, political, *ad hominem* and uninformed arguments will not be included, although it should be noted that these constitute the greater part of the published critical remarks regarding Sartre's work. It is the literary opus which is often criticized, by writers who assume that the plays, novels, short stories, etc., are definitive expressions of the author's philosophy. Thus the phrase, "Hell is other people" uttered by Garcin in *No Exit*, is taken to epitomize Sartre's attitude toward his fellow men, as if he had never written anything on the subject of being-for-others than this terse exclamation. Fortunately, a number of writers have addressed the *philosophical* writings and examined them of expertise; it is their criticism which will be examined here.

Some critics have reproached Sartre for claiming to use the phenomenological method, but in fact failing to do so. Obviously, if the criteria established by Husserl are applied to judgment of a so-called phenomenological work, Sartre's writing does not qualify. If one allows, however, that, like Husserl and Heidegger, like Merleau-Ponty and countless others, Sartre has a right to adapt the method to his own needs, to establish criteria which he believes to be appropriate, then it cannot very well be said that in this respect Sartre's philosophy is deficient. There may be some question as to the use of the term 'phenomenological' for one's own version of a method which was developed and named by someone else, but it is not within the scope of this study to enter into a discussion about that. Suffice it to quote an authoritative critic of Sartre, Varet, who says,

> If one sees in phenomenology not a simple recipe to be used for a definite type of problem, but rather a "mentality" susceptible of being opened on all the horizons of the "cultural life" of man, it is not to subscribe without criticism to a few magical formulas, it is to make efforts in the undertakings of the mind . . . that Sartre has always insisted on defining as "phenomenological" his philosophical enterprise, no one thinks of reproaching him for it.[1]

In addition to questions concerning the use of the term 'phenomenology,' one finds that criticism of Sartre's view of the Other falls into three major categories.[2] Some critics address his ontology directly. Others are concerned with the ethical implications of his ontology. Finally there are those whose chief interest lies in the social and political aspects of his philosophy. In reviewing the criticisms in this order, then, the emphasis will be placed on the comments specifically directed to the structures of being-for-others.

Ontology

Since the nexus of the structures of being in Sartre's system is the for-itself, it is to be expected that this notion would receive the greatest attention. To what extent is the for-itself really free? Can Sartre maintain with any seriousness that the for-itself is impersonal, unidentifiable with an _ego_? Can the for-itself be emptied of everything that is contaminated by _being_? At some point the ethical dimension overlaps the ontological. Suppose a man is constituted in a certain way, e.g., he exists within the limits created by the objectifying attitudes of the Other. To what extent is his moral behavior determined by this situation and the bounds it places on him?

It appears that, generally, the major criticisms of Sartre in one way or another call into question the extent to which man, or the human condition, or the for-itself, is free. Does existence precede essence, or does it not? To say, as does Desan,[3] that man's freedom, as described in **Being and Nothingness**, can be considered to be man's essence, so as to refute Sartre, using his own ideas, seems to skirt the issue of essence and to completely miss the central point of the argument about freedom. Rather, the question should be raised as to the truth of an assertion like, for example, the one made by Ortega y Gasset (sounding very much like Sartre) describing the "radical reality" of life.

> . . . circumstance always offers us different possibilities for acting, hence for being. This obliges us, like it or not, to exercise our freedom. We are forced to be free. Because of this, life is a permanent crossroads and constant perplexity. At every instant we have to choose whether in the next

instant or at some other future time we shall be he who does this or he who does that. Hence, each of us is incessantly choosing his "doing," hence his being.[4]

Jeanson expresses similarly what he believes Sartre means by freedom.

> When Sartre speaks to us about freedom, it is still a question in spite of certain appearances, of human freedom in contrast to the determinism of things; this liberty to which we are "condemned," we have to make our freedom, otherwise it will not be long before it becomes one more determinism. We *are* free, but that does not exempt us in any way from having to *make* ourselves free.[5]

Not everyone agrees with these writers of "existentialist persuasion" championed by Sartre. Olafson, who acknowledges his debt to Erik Erikson, points out that the notions of choice and decision apply to many important aspects of human life "only in a rather strained sense."[6] Does one really choose to love or trust another human being? For example, does the battered child choose to tell the judge that he wants to return home where he knows, in good faith, that he will continue to be abused? As Olafson says,

> It is certainly possible to choose not to perform the actions that are the natural expression of [love and trust]; and it is even possible to perform or to try to perform those actions even in the absence of the real feelings with which the latter are normally associated. It seems very likely however that any attempt to substitute a kind of volitional fiat for these feeling-states or, worse still, to transform the latter into volitional acts would produce at best a very unstable and imperfect facsimile of the "real thing."[7]

Whether or not a person is free to choose the mode in which he meets the Other is a question of paramount concern. In one sense, Sartre contends that the for-itself, caught, as it were, peeking through the keyhole of his world, must respond with shame, or fear, or both. "My original fall is the existence of the other," he says at one point, and later reiterates the thought when he declares, "Original Sin is my upsurge into a world where there are others" (EN 481). On the other hand, the structure of being-for-itself on which Sartre repeatedly insists is its total freedom to negate anything that is.

In a footnote of *Being and Nothingness*, Sartre states, after completing a description of the inevitable collapse of all attempts to resolve the subject-object conflict, "These considerations do not exclude the possibility of an ethics of deliverance and salvation. But this may be achieved only after a radical conversion which we cannot discuss here" (EN 484). According to Hazel Barnes, this statement explains how a person can be totally free at the same time that he is affected by the objectifying look of the Other. She claims that Sartre has stated explicitly that his analysis of interpersonal relations in *Being and Nothingness* applies only to relations *in bad faith* (emphasis mine). She does not make clear whether the footnote quoted above is the explicit statement regarding relations in bad faith (if so, one might wish for even more explicitness) or, if not, where or when the statement was made. I find the phrase "relations in bad faith" somewhat strange in the first place. It would be more in keeping with Sartrean theory to say that a person, in good or bad faith, enters into relation with the Other. Thus, there is the possibility of the Other's, in good or bad faith, entering into the same relation.[8] Since "relations in bad faith" does not distinguish clearly between which of the partners (both?) is/are in bad faith, it would seem to be infelicitous in this discussion.

There is an issue to be resolved which is even more fundamental. The tenability of the Sartrean ontological "structure" of the for-itself must be established before debating which qualities may be predicated about it. Whether or not Sartre can be saved from the charges that there are contradictions in the for-itself depends on one's willingness to go along with his system. For example, Desan has argued that it is necessary for Sartre to empty the for-itself by claiming that all its activities are contaminated by nonbeing in order to validate his system. Desan asserts that Sartre accomplishes this by means of sophistry and, sometimes, even error.

Varet has written[9] that *Being and Nothingness* is by and large a confirmation, with more precision and some rectification, of the demonstration of the structure of the phenomenological *cogito* which Sartre had already elaborated in the *Transcendence of the Ego*. There is some new material in *Being and Nothingness*, according to Varet, but it is relegated primarily to the Introduction and Conclusion. Why the emphasis on the *cogito*, why the effort in explicating its most hidden recesses? Because, Varet echoes Desan's observation, the *cogito* is indispensable to the architecture of the Sartrean ontology.

What Sartre tried to prove, as noted before, was that the entire ontological mass of *being* is anchored to the for-itself. The paradox of intentionality, as he views it, is that *being*, properly speaking, pertains uniquely to the objective externality of the in-itself. Consciousness is, then, the "outside" of things, the "emptiness" of the in-itself. It is of paramount importance that the for-itself is never construed, strange as the notion may appear, as existing for-itself, but rather, always as existing for the object of its intention.

Granting that "interrogation" supposes an absence of knowledge, Desan does not agree with Sartre's claim ". . . that this absence of knowledge is a form of non-being incarnated in consciousness itself." Because human consciousness is able to discern "what is and what is not but could be," he says, "it certainly does not follow that this consciousness itself is a non-being under any form whatsoever . . ."[10]

Concerning "negative judgement," Desan makes the same charge. If, after I have looked carefully and do not find Peter in the café, I conclude that he is not there, it is erroneous to describe the situation as "nonbeing" localized in the café or in my mind. It is, rather, a negative judgment--something which the human consciousness is capable of making.[11]

The third notion which, according to Sartre, is revelatory of nonbeing is destruction. As mentioned earlier, the house which has been painted *was* green only to a human witness. Similarly, an empty lot where a house once stood indicates *to a human witness*, that the house has since been destroyed. Jean Wahl has argued[12] that regardless of whether or not a human person witnessed the destruction of a planet during the pre-Cambrian period, it is not incorrect to assert that the planet was destroyed. Obviously, if one substitutes "the planet is extinct" for "the planet was destroyed," the difficulty is removed. Sartre objects merely to the choice of words, i.e., the verb 'destroy.' However, according to Desan, Jean Wahl has not addressed the principal issue, which is: ". . . does destruction imply the existence of a nonbeing in human consciousness?"[13] Desan, of course, says that it does not. He insists that human consciousness need not be a nonbeing in order to perceive change.

Varet believes that the problem is one of failure to distinguish between reflexive knowing of self and pre-reflexive existence of the *cogito*. If one stops at the phenomenal, there is no problem. Being "is" and the existential *cogito* prereflexively apprehends it. Only after a phenomenological reduction, which Varet points out is not obligatory (even without it we would apprehend "being" in *anguish*), does a reflexive movement bring into question the existence of the for-itself, and from there, the being of his existence.[12] Sartre would reiterate that the being of the existent, capable of interrogating being, is always only the in-itself."

The reason that so many commentators have taken issue with Sartre's description of the for-itself as totally devoid of being is, no doubt, the fact that such a claim leads him to assert that the *cogito*, the for-itself, is not identifiable with an ego, an "I." In opposition to Descartes, Kant, Hegel, and Husserl, he contends that there is no underlying entity, in human consciousness, which warrants one's saying, "I am" or "I think." Moreover, according to Sartre, the for-itself is impersonal, it is constituted as a relation with, a revelation of, a desire for an object, but in no case is there a necessary subject such as the Kantian synthetic unity of apperception. Desan and Grene seem outraged by this view. Varet accepts it as consistent with the ontology of Sartre. Phyllis Sutton Morris does more: she proposes to explain how Sartre's original description of the body and its role in human reality refutes Desan's arguments.[15]

Desan finds Sartre's rejection of "authentic reflection," and the substitution for it of the so-called "small" reflection (reflection without scissiparity, to use Sartre's terms) an act of philosophic leger-de-main. Authentic reflection, it will be remembered, is the act whereby a person is explicitly conscious of what he knows. "The inevitable result of authentic reflection," Desan points out, "is the presence of the Ego. I consider *myself* knowing the table."[16] Thus, in order to avoid this "inevitable" result, Sartre is forced to do away with authentic reflection, and he introduces the variations on the theme of reflection mentioned above.[17]

Desan argues that Sartre himself recognizes that the prereflexive consciousness has *meaning* only because there is an ulterior reflection. Only an ulterior, or authentic, reflection, could know about the prereflexive cogito. As Desan sees it,

> Sartre's seven hundred pages of phenomenological description are a result of his own constant, permanent and inquisitive reflection: it is because he himself has observed carefully what appears in his prereflexive Cogito by means of authentic reflection that he has been able to expose his view and to tell us that . . . there is no Ego! His Ego was present all the time.[18]

Grene sees this differently. Pointing to Polanyi's notion of "subsidiary awareness," a nonthetic foundation of "the most plainly inductive, positional (or, in Polanyi's language, focal) awareness of an object,"[19] she argues that nonthetic awareness need not be, indeed is not, as Sartre claims, consciousness (of) self. Rather, she considers the nonthetic ground of consciousness to be a set of clues on which a person relies, from which the person moves,

> . . . in order to make out, through them, the outlines, the meaning of [his] focal object in the world, not of [himself]. The subsidiary is indeed interiorized, it is mine, but it is not I, or no more so than is the focal object I comprehend through it and with its aid. It is the crutch I lean on to advance out there into and with the world.[20]

Grene's position, then, seems not only to contradict Desan's, but it does so in finding that Sartre insists too much on reflexion and not enough on the outward direction of consciousness. Whereas Desan sees in reflecting about reflection evidence of an ego, Grene simply notes that Sartre's search for the being of the percipient leads him to a nonreflective awareness (of) self as a nonsubstantial absolute.

Desan advances a second argument against an impersonal for-itself which is not much more convincing than the first. There is an "intimate and unshakable conviction that I am," he argues,[21] and insists that this overwhelming belief cannot be destroyed by even the most subtle dialectic of Sartre. It applies equally to Hume's elimination of the objective indentity of the self. Desan adds in a footnote,

> If the For-itself is "relation towards . . .," and if relation supposes a terminus a quo as well as a terminus ad quem, the result is that just as the Being-in-itself is something, so the For-itself hides something, namely the Ego. It is I who know the world, it is I who desire the world, it is I who choose and it is I who negate, it is I who desire the glass of water.[22]

thus appearing to illustrate his own contention that "this unmistakable evidence "[that I am something, and that this something is really existent]" may be difficult to justify.[23] It is indeed difficult, it seems to me, to justify a claim by merely repeating it in a crescendo of alternative phrases.

Phyllis Sutton Morris makes clear that Sartre does not deny that "I am," that "I am the center of my acts," that "a relation requires a terminus a quo as well as a terminus ad quem; but it does not follow from any of these points . . . that the I is an immaterial person-substance or ego. Sartre says that the body is the 'center of action' (BN 320)."[24] It will not be necessary to elaborate on Sartre's explanation of the body's role in perception or action. If the expository section of this study does not provide sufficient detail, the reader is referred to Being and Nothingness-- and/or to the commentaries by Salvan and Catalano. The fact is that the body is a necessary condition of all action, as has been shown, and therefore the need for a transcendental I is not indicated on the basis of Desan's argument.

The most serious charge which Desan makes is his last set of arguments, wherein he claims that an ego is necessary to provide the unifying connection of our experience in terms both of time and of spatiality.[25] Again, he seems to ignore what Sartre has said about the body as the subject term of conscious relations, Morris points out, and she adds,

> The body can provide a unified subject in single acts of awareness; it can provide both a spatial and a chronological unity. The body is in the spatial center of situations, and it persists as a subject from birth to death. This point does not seem to require elaboration.[26]

According to Morris, the arguments advanced by Scanlon,[27] which also assume that the underlying entity in locutions like *I think* or *I am* must be a transcendental ego, fare no better than those of Desan. Scanlon, it appears, has also overlooked the fact that the body-subject fulfills all of the conditions of what he claims to be ". . . a continuing subjective unity: a subject with individual characteristics and a 'concrete intentional life' which is related to a continuing world of meanings," without the need of adding a transcendental ego.

Varet concedes that there is a problem of "me" (the French *moi*) in all of this discussion, but certainly not one of *I*. Even the problem of "me" should not be over-emphasized, for with the help of the prereflexive *cogito* alone, most of the questions can be answered. He says,

> To look for being in the depths of the *cogito*, is not to step back from the existential condition of the "human reality;" it is rather settling from the start in the heart of this intentional existence in order to search there for the secret of its ontological access . . . . The question. . .

is one of form: how is there being here? What are, from the side ob being the 'conditions of possibility' of an intentional life of the consciousness?--Where does one see that these questions refer initially to the being of an "I"?[28]

There are numerous other arguments which aim at uncovering one weakness or another in Sartre's ontology. To present them here and to note their own inconsistencies with the work they ostensibly discredit would serve no useful purpose. As stated earlier, Sartre's ontology resists serious criticism if one accepts his idiosyncratic view of being, nothingness, and human consciousness. The criticisms examined above are perhaps the most cogent, and have been cited for this reason as much as to elucidate further the exposition of Sartre's ideas. There are some observations still to be examined--not on Sartre's ontology per se, but nonetheless these are informative. The next section will be devoted to them in order to complete the criticism of Sartre's point of view.

Ethics

Although Sartre promised to write an existentialist ethics, he seems to have decided against it as early as 1950.[29] His reasons for abandoning the project have to do with the political climate at that time. According to Simone de Beauvoir, he said, "The ethical attitude appears when technological and social conditions render positive conduct impossible. Ethics is a collection of idealist devices to help you live the life which poverty of resources and lack of techniques impose upon you."[30] He made it clear, then, that he had no intention of ever writing the ethics which he had once declared he would. Why then, do so many writers attack his ethics? Why are his critics so intent on drawing attention to ostensible weaknesses and flaws in his ontology, as evidenced by ethical implications which allegedly follow from it?

Sartre is at least partly responsible for this problem. He had promised to write a book " on the ethical level" which would, among other things, elaborate on some points in *Being and Nothingness*. Since he failed to do so, many questions remain unresolved. Furthermore, his literary works clearly take an ethical stance which the author nowhere repudiates. If anything, he defends the ethical implications of his literary corpus on the basis of his philosophical writings. Therefore, the critic who addresses *No Exit, The Flies, The Roads to Freedom, The Devil and the Good Lord*, to name but the most applicable, touches directly on Sartre's ethics, or, to say the least, the ethical implications of Sartre's writings which he never repudiated. Finally, there is a sense in which it is impossible to distinguish the ontological from the ethical aspects of his work. It is this last observation which accounts for the numerous writers who comment on Sartre's ontology as if it were a work on ethics.

For example, Marjorie Grene concedes that Sartre's argument, on his own premises, on the foundation of the *cogito* alone, is irresistible. Nevertheless, she wants to question it. One cannot lightly dismiss the testimony of experience, she points out, such as "the rare but still indubitable experience of mutual understanding, of the reciprocal look of peers; or the look of mother and infant, where the one protects and *the other* is protected."[31] She adduces further empirical evidence to call into doubt Sartre's pessimistic conclusion that all interpersonal relations are necessarily conflict situations. She cites the well documented fact that infants deprived of a family setting develop more slowly, and ". . . deprived of some simulation at least of an affectionate initiation by Others into the human world, become retarded perhaps beyond recall."[32]

Sartre fails to _see_ the counterexamples, according to Grene, because of what she calls his phenomenological or empirical narrowness. By her account, Sartre has made three significant errors: (1) he confines the prereflexive _cogito_ to consciousness (of) self (Piaget has described children who can do arithmetic without being able to say how they do it, thus ostensibly illustrating a nonthetic consciousness that carries a person away from self to the world), (2) he resists the Heideggerian insight that being with others is an essential aspect of being oneself, and (3) his concept of a _pure detached instant_ as the model for the existence of consciousness is illusory, and so is his notion of _pure freedom_. Grene contends that social time and social space are already presupposed as necessary conditions for the existence of the for-itself, and that human freedom is never _instantaneous_ and complete, but rather entails the internalization of standards.[33]

Mary Warnock also criticizes the possibility of an ethical theory of this vast, unbounded freedom. She asserts that there is a contradiction in _Being and Nothingness_ to which Sartre does not pay enough attention. She asks,

> How can we reconcile the belief that we are absolutely free to choose whatever life we want, to be what we want, with the belief that in our dealings with others we are committed entirely to an unending conflict from which there is no escape? . . . If ethics . . . is concerned with the fitting together of the interests and choices of one person with those of another, there is no way into the subject at all if our aim is _necessarily_ to dominate the other person and subordinate his freedom to our own.[34]

There is another point which Warnock finds objectionable in Sartre's theory, and that is his claim that nothing per se is absolutely valuable. To believe that there are things good in themselves, or that some things are good because their consequences are desirable, is to be in bad faith and, specifically, to view matters in the Spirit of Seriousness.[35] And yet, if for human reality, to be is to choose oneself, and if in so doing one assigns values to things, as is necessarily the case when one chooses to pursue one project rather than another, then, it would appear, there must be values that are transcendent, that are to be discovered. On this issue, Buber found Sartre's point of view to be almost naïve.[36] However, beyond the ostensible naïveté there are serious disagreements between Sartre and Buber on the source(s) of values. The divergent views of both authors will be seen more clearly in the section which examines Buber's point of view.

Warnock rightly insists that Sartre cannot "have it both ways." If, in choosing themselves, men disclose values, if they choose what they judge is worth choosing, then men are necessarily moral beings. And if men are ontologically moral, there must be more than Sartre's "negative ethics" to guide their way: "negative" because it enjoins men to take full responsibility for what they do, and spells out the pitfalls of bad faith in resolving difficult dilemmas, but fails to provide positive criteria for authentic moral choices. Sartre's reply to Warnock would be that indeed man is a moral being, he must choose whom and what he wants to be, and in so doing discloses value; but his choice must always be free, it must always be his own, and if there are to be criteria for authentic moral choice, these must be invented by him and not provided to him ready-made by society. "Ontology cannot itself formulate moral prescriptions," Sartre says, "it deals only with what is, and it is not possible to draw imperatives from its indicatives." (EN 720)

It is at the point, where Sartre insists that man is free to choose himself, that interpersonal relations are ontologically conflict situations and that one cannot derive, as it were, an "ought" from an "is," that the ontological blurs with the ethical. Sartre sounds as if he is saying that we *ought to be* authentic rather than act in bad faith, that we *ought to* reinvent values rather than obscure all our goals in order to free ourselves from anguish.

Olafson questions the possibility of a theory of moral obligation when views such as Sartre's, wherein the human reality is primarily the source of ultimate moral conflict, dominate a theory of being-for-others. According to Sartre, Olafson claims, there is hardly a possibility of genuine mutuality among human beings. This claim echoes Grene's, Warnock's, and those of numerous other commentators on Sartre. Moreover, in all of Sartre's novels, plays, and short stories, very few images of dialogical relationship are portrayed, whereas the literary characters who exemplify existence in bad faith crowd the pages of these works.

Community

In order to comment on Sartre's viewpoint regarding groups, in contrast to the examination of his notions on interpersonal relations, i.e., the self and *others* in contrast to the self and the Other, one must abandon the pages of *Being and Nothingness*. It is in the *Critique de la raison dialectique*,[37] that there appears for the first time a serious and elaborate description of the ontology of the social and political organization of groups. To be sure, the author refers occasionally to his earlier philosophical work. He is especially careful not to contradict any of his basic phenomenological claims regarding the for-itself. In his descriptions of the various types of groups which typify modern society, for example, Sartre insistently stresses the importance of the individual. Nevertheless, in his writings in 1960 the emphasis has shifted, and it is here that one must look for Sartre's concept of community.

Burkle has argued[38] that the "ideal" form of social unity, for Sartre, is the "group-in-fusion" especially because such a group is "more in accord with the ontology of human freedom: it provides a more creative outlet for human energies, permits individual choice to have greater impact on the course of public affairs, and is more hospitable to individual diversity."[39]

In order to evaluate Burkle's claim, it is necessary to summarize Sartre's distinctions of the various types of groups. It should be remembered, however, that on this level, Sartre is no longer engaged in phenomenological ontology, but rather is describing society as he views it. It is made up of divers groupings which overlap frequently, and it is in full knowledge of his ontological structure of the human reality, which is the fundamental unit, that the various types of groups must be understood.

In the group-in-series, the individuals who compose it, although they share an interest (e.g., waiting for a subway, attending class in the same building of a university, watching a performance in a theater), interact only minimally. "Solitude" and "interchangeability" characterize the group-in-series, which affords a minimum of individuality to its members. In contrast, the group-in-fusion is characterized by solidarity, a common purpose, which nevertheless allows for the individuality of each member and even enhances it, as each contributor to the common cause is prized for his role. The paradigm which Sartre cites for the group-in-fusion is the Parisian mob which stormed the Bastille in 1789. In response to the dehumanizing "seriality" of life at that time, poor, oppressed, desperate citizens of Paris fused into a group which saw no other way out of their misery than to fight together.

When the group-in-fusion succeeds in its praxis,[40] there sets in, sooner or later, a decreased zeal and need for venture. It is at this point that the group-under-oath may become manifest. This particular group resembles the group-in-fusion in that its members are actively aware of sharing a common project with each other, but it is more ordered, routinized, almost institutionalized. There is no longer an external enemy to combat, and the members of the group begin to fear an internal threat, those members who place their own interest before the perpetuation of the group. The group is "under oath" at this point. Individuals are bound to the community. Sartre cautions that this is not a form of social contract, for there is no tacit consent of the governed. Rather, Burkle explains, its validity depends on "a habituated sense of duty, a socially conditioned acceptance of the jurisdiction of the group over the life of the individual."[41]

The fourth basic social form which Sartre describes is the **Institution**. This type of organization reflects the stage of a society wherein self-perpetuation as the paramount concern of the members has been legitimized and institutionalized. Responsibilities have been divided and assigned to various agencies, and, equally important, mechanisms have been established to defend against the disruptions of deviant members. Sartre admits that in the **institution** there is less room for individuality, but the survival of the society is ensured. In the group-in-fusion security and survival are not guaranteed. In the **institution**, an exchange has been transacted, as it were, to ensure these at the cost of the loss of some freedom.

As noted earlier, Sartre does not offer these four categories as ontological structures of social being. Nor does he claim to be reporting the result of empirical social researches. He is merely describing certain social phenomena as these appear to his intuition. What significance, then, can be ascribed to this idiosyncratic view of society, which appears at times to be superficial, at other times to be "strained" in order to fit previously established categories (e.g., the project of the for-itself and the praxis of the group-in-fusion), and at still other times to be oriented politically?

According to Burkle, Sartre's description of the groups of social unity presents the only positive comment on interpersonal relationship in all of his philosophical writings. If Burkle is right, and I believe he is, the "ideal" of social unity is very significant indeed. Limited though Sartre's vision of the possibility of mutuality in human relations may be, it is nevertheless expressed here, in his "later" work, ready to refute his critics who claim that Sartrean existentialism is monological. As Burkle describes it, Sartre sounds almost optimistic:

> The magic instant of the surging group-in-fusion is as close as Sartre's humanity will ever get to heaven. In the enthusiasm to breach the walls of the Bastille, the grinding pains of the real world are transcended: hunger is forgotten, death is overcome. The other man, my enemy, is suddenly so much my friend, so close to me that I literally cannot tell where he begins and I end. Here, in the moment of fusion, Sartre finds the means to escape the nightmarish "Look" of the "Other" which he vainly struggled to overcome in nonpolitical ways in <u>Being and Nothingness</u>.[42]

The Other in the later writings of Sartre is then different from the Other in his ontology. A considerable number of adjustments would have to be made in order to adapt his ontology to a view whereby man can enter into genuine dialogue with his fellow man, as happens in the fleeting moments of the group-in-fusion. For Martin Buber, as the following chapter will show, the ontological Other is none other than the person with whom each of us is able to enter into dialogue.

Footnotes

1. Varet, *L'Ontologies de Sartre*, pp. 44-45.

2. The best sources of bibliographical material for this purpose are Michel Contat and Michel Rybalka, *Les Ecrits de Sartre* (Paris: Gallimard, 1970), François and Claire Lapointe, *Jean-Paul Sartre and His Critics: An International Bibliography (1938-1975)* (Ohio: Bowling Green State University, Philosophy Documentation Center, 1975).

3. Wilfred Desan, *The Tragic Finale* (Cambridge: Harvard University Press, 1954).

4. José Ortega y Gasset, *Man and People*, trans. Willard R. Trask (New York: W. W. Norton & Co., 1957), p. 58.

5. Francis Jeanson, *Le Problème moral et la pensée de Sartre* (Paris: Editions du Seuil, 1965). p. 27.

6. Frederick A. Olafson, *Principles and Persons: An Ethical Interpretation of Existentialism* (Baltimore: Johns Hopkins Press, 1967), p. 248.

7. Ibid.

8. This idea, as will be shown below, is one which Buber explains in minute detail.

9. Varet, *L'Ontologie de Sartre*, pp. 82-83.

10. Desan, *Tragic Finale*, p. 140.

11. Desan argues that consciousness ". . . is (or has) a faculty which is able to compare, to divide, to abstract, to construct and to reconstruct, to go backward in time, to foresee, to view its 'possibles,' and so on, and hence to formulate interrogative and negative judgements." Ibid., p. 141.

12. In *Deucalien*, 1:47 (1946) as reported by Desan, Ibid., p. 142.

13. Ibid., p. 143.

14. In view of this interpretation by Varet, it would seem that Desan, Wahl, Grene and other critics of *Being and Nothingness* argue somewhat on the basis of their own, distorted, notions regarding Sartre's ontology.

15. Phyllis Sutton Morris, *Sartre's Concept of a Person: An Analytic Approach* (Amherst: University of Mass. Press, 1976).

16. Desan, *Tragic Finale*, p. 150.

17. In addition to 'small' and 'without scissiparity,' Sartre uses the designations *une réflexion complice,* and *une réflexion du coin de l'oeil*. Ibid.

18. Ibid. (Suspension points in original.)

19. Grene, *Sartre*, pp. 120-21.

20. Ibid., p. 121.

21. Desan, *Tragic Finale,* p. 151.

22. Ibid., p. 152.

23. Ibid., p. 151.

24. Morris, *Sartre's Concept of a Person*, p. 40.

25. Desan, *Tragic Finale*, p. 152-53.

26. Morris, *Sartre's Concept of a Person*, p. 41. There are other points which the author does elaborate upon, namely, Sartre's view of a person's character (with reference to a fundamental project or ideal self), and Sartre's objection to the "spatial image underlying the container view of consciousness."

27. John D. Scanlon, "Consciousness, the Streetcar, and the Ego: *Pro* Husserl, *Contra* Sartre," *Philosophical Forum*, no. 2 (Spring 1971), p. 350, cited in Morris, *Sartre's Concept of a Person*, p. 39.

28. Varet, *L'Ontologie de Sartre*, p. 92.

29. See Hazel Barnes, *An Existentialist Ethics* (New York: Alfred A. Knopf, 1967), p. 29.

30. Simone de Beauvoir, *La Force des Choses* (Paris: Gallimard, 1963), p. 218, as cited by Barnes, ibid., p. 30.

31. Grene, *Sartre*, p. 154 (emphasis mine).

32. Ibid. this particular point is taken up by Buber, as will be shown below, in his elaboration of the development of the infant's ability to enter into relation with its mother.

33. It seems to me that here, like so many of Sartre's critics, Grene overlooks the key concept of *facticity* which provides an adequate background, as it were, for the internalized standards of the for-itself.

34. Mary Warnock, *Existentialist Ethics* (New York: St. Martins Press, 1967), p. 47. As the quotation from de Beauvoir indicates, it is precisely for the reason given by Warnock that Sartre abandoned the project to write an ethics. As for our "aim to dominate the other person, etc.," Sartre does

not claim this to be a moral choice recommended to man, but rather a reality of his being-for-others.

35. Which, Sartre says,". . . has double characteristics: it considers values as transcendent, given independent of human subjectivity, and it transfers the quality of desirable from the ontological structure of things to their simple material constitution. . . . The result of the serious attitude, which as we know rules the world, is to cause the symbolic values of things to be drunk in by their empirical idiosyncracy as ink by a blotter: it puts forward the opacity of the desired object and posts it in itself as a desirable irreducible" (EN 721).

36. See p. 179 below.

37. Jean-Paul Sartre, *Critique de la raison dialectique* (Paris: Gallimard, 1960). (Hereafter CRD.)

38. Howard R. Burkle, "Sartre's "Ideal" of Social Unity," in *Sartre*, ed. Mary Warnock, Modern Studies in Philosophy, Anchor Books (Garden City, N.Y.: Doubleday & Co., 1971), pp. 315-336.

39. Ibid., p. 317.

40. Burkle explains that this term, as used by Sartre in relation to the group, means essentially what 'project' denotes for the individual in *Being and Nothingness*, i.e., 'purposive' activity. Ibid., p. 318n.

41. Ibid., p. 325.

42. Ibid., pp. 335-36.

PART THREE

CHAPTER IV

THE OTHER IN THE ONTOLOGY OF BUBER

For the examination of Sartre's concept of the Other it was methodologically convenient to refer to that particular chapter in his essay on phenomenological ontology which is devoted specifically to this concept. To explicate Buber's ontology as regards the Other, one can find no such singular and specific source of information. Instead, the theory must be pieced together from ideas which are expressed in a plurality of writings. Nevertheless, it is certain that a consistent, systematic view of the self and the Other pervades the ontology of Martin Buber, and it is the aim of this chapter to examine this particular view.

The most useful work in which to begin the analysis of Buber's concept of the other is his book *I and Thou*.[1] This brief work was written at about midpoint in the author's life. According to Buber, in writing *I and Thou* he was impelled by an inner necessity to express a vision which had come to him again and again since his youth (IT 123). In the years that followed the publication of the book, it became apparent that amplification was required, and so Buber returned throughout the rest of his life to the clarification of the vision. The ideas of *I and Thou* are central, then, to the philosophy of the author in more ways than one.

I and Thou

The style of *I and Thou* is mystical, poetic, often difficult to comprehend. Several probing commentaries have been written on this work, among which Robert E. Wood's *Martin Buber's Ontology: An Analysis of I and Thou*[2], and Maurice Friedman's *Martin Buber: The Life of Dialogue*,[3] stand out as the most comprehensive. The recently published work by Rivka Horwitz, *Buber's Way to I and Thou: An Historical Analysis of the First Publication of Martin Buber's Lectures "Religion als Gengenwart"*[4] is a painstaking account of the development of Buber's philosophy as it advanced from ideas presented to students in various lecture series to their final formulation in published form. The author's own early work provides rich background, religious and philosophical, by reference to which the ideas can be grasped more clearly. Since many of the later works were written expressly to elucidate the original notions, these too are necessary for a thorough understanding of "dialogical philosophy." With the help of commentaries to explain obscure formulations, and with the benefit of the author's own elaboration, the task of interpreting his ideas into a systematic context is made somewhat manageable. The vast literature on Buber's thought[5] renders the task more manageable still.

"All real living is meeting," says Buber in *I and Thou*,[6] and thereby expresses the central idea of his philosophy. The impasse between subjectivity and objectivity, which Husserl saw as a major problem,[7] and the tension between the spontaneous immediacy of life and the detached and deliberative character of spirit,"[8] which Cassirer viewed as the central problem of philosophy in his day, are resolved by Buber's notion of an ontological relation prior to these dichotomies. This prior relation, Presence, binds subject and object together in a region which Buber calls 'there-in-between'(*dazwischen*). In this same region, there is unity of life and spirit.

The relation between things, especially between the self and the Other, is the ground of their existence. As a person takes his stand in the world he expresses his identity by means of the primary words, I-Thou, or, I-It. These primary words may or may not be uttered linguistically. In either case, the <u>Grundwort</u> is a reference to the Other, that which meets man, and the determinant of the primary word is not the Other who is over against him, not the object, but rather the manner in which man relates himself to the objects.

"To man the world is twofold," Buber states at the beginning of <u>I and Thou,</u> "in accordance with his twofold attitude." Man's attitude is twofold, in accordance with the twofold nature of the primary words he speaks. These words are not isolated, Buber explains, but rather they are combined words. 'I-Thou' and 'I-It' do not signify things, they intimate relations. When 'I-Thou' is said, the I is different from the I which speaks the primary words 'I-It'. 'I-Thou' can only be said with the whole being. 'I-It' can never be said with the whole being (IT 3).

Buber does not neglect the epistemological problems raised by the claims made at the beginning of <u>I and Thou</u>. The world, man, language, sense phenomena, all receive extensive articulation in one or another of Buber's essays. But the form of <u>I and Thou</u> is such that the reader must discover as he goes along, with only the help of aphoristic sentences orchestrated in divers contexts, the ideas which the author wants to convey.

For example, the difference between the I-Thou relation and the I-It relation is stated concisely in the opening pages of <u>I and Thou</u>, but refinements, elaboration and illustrations recur throughout the rest of the book. In Part One, the development of this theme is limited to the sphere between man and man. In Part Two, the relation between man and nature is examined. In Part Three, the author sets forth his view of the meeting between man and God, the Eternal

Thou. There is much to be learned in this last section which applies to the relations described in the fist section. Similarly, the ideas in Part Three cannot be comprehended before a thorough assimilation of the first part.

The I-Thou relation corresponds to one of the two basic movements of man, namely, turning toward the Other (_Hinwendung_). In this movement, the Other is viewed as wholly in itself. This relation is possible only because man can distance himself from his own givenness, he can transcend the immanent. Selfhood is enhanced, i.e., it is detached, as it were, from the totality of things, in proportion to the awareness of otherness. According to Wood, "Revelation of the Other-in-totality presupposes and grounds, in a simultaneous mutual act, self-in-totality."[9]

The Other basic movement of man, reflexion, or bending back toward oneself (_Rückbiegung_), develops into an I-It relation, whereby the Other is considered to be an object for one's use. The person confronted is not viewed as _other_, but as _other-for-me_. And since the Other is not wholly made present, neither is the self.

The language used to describe the I-Thou relation is particularly eloquent. When a person utters, Thou, Buber says, he does not address

> . . . a nature able to be experienced and described, a loose bundle of named qualities. But with no neighbor, and whole in himself, he is _Thou_ and fills the heavens. . . . So long as the heaven of _Thou_ is spread out over me the winds of causality cower at my heels, and the whirlpool of fate stays its course. I do not experience the man to whom I say _Thou_. But I take my stand in relation to him, in the sanctity of the primary word.... Even if the man to whom I say _Thou_ is not aware of it in the midst of his experience,

yet relation may exist. For _Thou_ is more than _It_ realizes. (IT 8-9)

To describe the world of I-It, the author employs more precise, less figurative speech. Here, in this "world," activities are goal directed. Man _experiences_ the Other, or simply, otherness. A person sees, thinks, imagines, wills, etc. These activities have an intentional structure, characteristic of subject-object relations. Whereas in the I-Thou relation, the undivided self encounters the undivided Other, in the I-It relation, there is an inner and an outer secret and open experience which affects the person and his partner.

Grete Schaeder points out[10] that for Buber, I-speaking and I-existence are the same. If a person greets the world with the powers of the mind, there is a consciousness of something, and a separation of subject and object is involved. In this manner knowledge is created, out of which the world of time and space is structured: the world view of science which men can communicate with each other. This is the world of It.[11] In the world of Thou, a person takes his stand with his unmediated being. The I-Thou relation, according to Schaeder, ". . . is nothing but pure Presentness, limitless and incomparable: everything else lives in its light."

It is from relational events that a person's self-consciousness is gradually developed. In the developmental stages of children, and in primitive people, the Thou world exists in a natural, primal form. Buber cites examples of primitive people's expressions, in which the relational event is recorded, which correspond to our more "highly developed" conceptual communication. Following the formulation of Edward Sapir, but protesting that he cannot go along with the general basic view of that writer, Buber points out that word compounds in modern thinking are residues of an earlier stage of language. Some of these word compounds are preserved in several unrelated languages, e.g., the Eskimo and the

Algonquin, both so-called polysynthetic or holophrastic systems of communication.

In these languages, Buber states,

> The unit of speech with which one builds is not the word but the sentence. This is a structure that in its fully developed form exhibits components of three different kinds. Two of them, the so-called core element and the formal elements, both the modal as well as the personal, can also emerge as independent. Not so the element of the third kind, which might be designated as preponderantly suffixes. They appear exclusively in their serious function, but it is they that properly make possible the form of the sentence.[12]

Language is often referred to as Buber elaborates on the realm of "there-between." In I and Thou, he had already illustrated his claim that the speech of "primitive" people reflects an awareness of relation which is prior to that of their meager stock of objects (IT 18). The equivalent of our "far away" in Zulu is, "There where someone cries out: 'O mother, I am lost.'" The Fuegian, Buber notes, have a word which means, "they stare at one another, each waiting for the other to volunteer to do what both wish, but are not able to do." In contradistinction to our worn-out formulas used in greetings, Buber points to the original conferring of power which used to be expressed by "Hail!," the "ever fresh Kaffir greeting, with its direct bodily relation, "I see you!," or with its ridiculous and sublime American variant, "Smell me!." (IT 18) In his essay, "The Word that is Spoken," (KM 10-20) Buber presents further arguments to strengthen his claim that language is "living speech" between man and man.

That relation is prior to individuation Buber attempts to show not only through his analysis of language, but in his essays on art, the theatre, and religion. But in order to penetrate more deeply into his ontology as regards the other, it is more productive to focus on the poles (as he tends to designate the partners in relation) and this can best be accomplished by a close examination of the author's concepts of the only two possible types of relation.

I-Thou and I-It

The two possible types of relation are not a matter of conscious choice on the part of an individual. Such choice would presuppose an ontologically prior ego who could deliberate on the manner in which he might enter into relation. Buber maintains that such deliberation would necessarily lead one to the world of I-It, but besides, there is no *cogito* capable of deliberation, as it were, in a vacuum.

The I-Thou relation is primal. By this, Buber claims that in primitive speech, in art, in a new-born infant, in man's relation with God, the unmediated "whole being" of a person is expressed, from which subsequently an I-consciousness can separate itself and only then does the I-It relation become possible. The young child offers perhaps the clearest illustration of this notion. In its prenatal stage, the child is naturally united with its mother in more ways than one. He comes into the world with an impulse for relation throughout the rest of its life. Says Buber of the infant,

> But the effort to establish relation comes first--the hand of the child arched out so that what is over against him may nestle under it; second is the actual relation, a saying of *Thou* without words, in the state preceding the word-form; the thing, like the *I*, is produced late, arising after the original experiences have been split asunder and the connected partners separated. In the beginning is relation--as category of being,

readiness, grasping form, mould for the soul; it is the _a priori_ of relation, _the inborn Thou_. (IT 27)

The It-world is grasped in time and space by consciousness which has secured for it a coherent and ordered form. The world of Thou is not set in a time-space context. After a relational event has run its course, Buber laments, "the particular Thou _is bound_ to become an It." (IT 33) The particular _It_, on the other hand may or may not become a Thou. The It-World is more secure. It is the world in which man _must_ live, in which man finds "encitements and excitements, activity and knowledge." (IT 34) In contrast, the world of Thou presents "strange lyric and dramatic episodes, seductive and magical, but tearing us away to dangerous extremes, loosening the well-tried context, leaving more questions than satisfaction behind them, shattering security." (IT 34) One is tempted to remain permanently in the world of It. Many people do. It is not possible to live in the bare present, Buber says, but it is possible indeed to live in the bare past, wherein life may be organized. To do so, one needs but fill each moment with experiencing and using (IT 34). But the sacrifice is great, to say the least. For, says Buber,

> . . . in all the seriousness of truth, hear this: without _It_ man cannot live. But he who lives with _It_ alone is not a man. (IT 34)

This quotation, and other aphorisms which appear throughout the pages of _I and Thou_, become clear as one reads later material published by the author. Several essays particularly are essential to his thought. Of these, "Dialogue" is the most vital.

Dialogue

It is ironic that the term 'dialogue' has been adopted by demagogues, advertisers, propagandists and other persons, who in one sense wish the true meaning of the term to be understood yet who do not intend to enter into dialogue should the opportunity present itself. Buber had reintroduced the term into philosophy to denote in concrete images the stance that is taken by persons in the I-Thou relation. The description in the book, *I and Thou*, had been too theoretical, perhaps too mystical, in any case somewhat difficult to grasp. The essay "Dialogue" (BMM 1-39) was intended to "clarify the 'dialogical' principle, . . . to illustrate it and to make precise its relation to essential spheres of life." (BMM XI) The essay includes several examples of situations similar in form to those which had been offered in *Being and Nothingness* to illustrate the conflict which is inevitable when persons "meet." In "Dialogue," however, these meetings are characterized not by conflict but rather, more often than not, by genuine encounter. For example, two persons sit opposite one another on a train. They don't know each other, do not look at one another. They are not in one another's confidence. But if dialogue is to take place, one look suffices. As Buber describes the moment,

> And now--let us imagine that this is one of the hours which succeed in bursting asunder the seven iron bands about our heart--imperceptibly the spell is lifted . . . where unreserve has ruled, even wordlessly, between men, the word of dialogue has happened sacramentally. (BMM 4)

Another anecdote relates a visit Buber once received while he was in a mystical trance. an unknown young man had come to the renowned thinker, somewhat as a youth seeking the advice of an oracle. Although the trance had been interrupted, Buber was friendly. He conversed openly and attentively with the young man. However, Buber laments, he failed to guess the questions which the young man had not been able to articulate. Not long after, it was learned that the young man had died, perhaps a suicide. He had come to Buber, not for a chat, but for a decision. He had sought reassurance that life has meaning—but failed to obtain it from the man whose *presence* would have reassured him. This event is described by Buber as his "conversion." Since then, he says,

> I have given up the "religious" which is nothing but the exception, extraction, exaltation, ecstasy; or it has given me up. I possess nothing but the everyday out of which I am never taken . . . I know no fullness but each mortal hour's fullness of claim and responsibility. Though far from being equal to it, yet I know that in the claim *I* am claimed and may respond in responsibility and know *who* speaks and demands a response. (BMM 14, emphasis mine)

Martin Buber was not brought up an "observant" Jew. Later on he could not bring himself to consciously become observant. The spontaneity was lacking, and Buber felt that man's relationship with God is a private affair. He did not deprecate the value of institutionalized religion. He found great import in transmitting, from generation to generation, all the spiritual, moral, metaphysical and historical teachings of the great thinkers. In 1924, with Franz Rosenzweig, Buber undertook the project of translating the Old Testament from Hebrew into German. The resultant work, according to Eugen Biser,[13] is on a par with the Lutheran Bible and these two works are said to have no peer in the German language. Several other major biblical studies, __Königtum Gottes__ (1932), __Der Glaube der Propheten__ (1940), __Moses__ (1945), __Zwei Glaubensweisen__ (1950) __Gottesfinsternis__ (1953) and __Sehertum__ (1955), established Buber as a monumental figure in Jewish religious literature.

Another situation, described by Buber in the form of a tale, relates that a man inspired by God once left the earth and wandered into the vast waste. He knocked at the gates of mystery and when asked, "What do you want?," he declared that he had been proclaiming the praise of God in the ears of mortals but they were deaf to him. "So I come to you that you yourself may hear me and reply," he said. But from within there came a cry, "Turn back. Here is no ear for you. I have sunk my hearing in the deafness of mortals." (BMM 15) Thus dialogue is primarily between person and person.

As in *I and Thou*, Buber speaks of basic movements in "Dialogue." The basic movement of dialogue is the turning toward the Other with the body, of course, but also "in the requisite measure with the soul," in that a person directs all his attention to his partner. The basic movement of the life of monologue is reflexion. Buber makes clear that reflexion is something different from egoism and egotism--these can be added, he says, but they are not integral to reflexion. Rather, he defines this movement as the withdrawal from accepting with one's essential being another person in his particularity--a particularity which cannot be circumscribed by the circle of one's own self, which cannot be immanent in one's own soul.

All art is from its origin essentially dialogue. Music, architecture, sculpture, all beckon to an ear, an eye, the touch, which is not the artist's own. The all "say" something which can be "said" only in this one language. Thought, on the other hand, would seem to be more closely associated with the life of monologue. Buber questions the philosophers who say that in "thought . . . pure subject separates itself from the concrete person in order to establish and stabilize a world for itself." (BMM 26) He recalls that Plato repeatedly called thinking a voiceless colloquy of the soul with itself. But this, Buber contends, is not the true arising of the thought. In the stages of the growth of a thought, he says, the thinker does not address himself, but rather the "basic relation in face of which he has to answer for his insight." More important than the empirical self to which the thinker must answer is the "genius," the spirit he is intended to become, the image-self. Even this "self" does not satisfy, however. There appears the longing for testing in the sphere of dialogue. The thinker needs an Other. Buber quotes Wilhilm von Humboldt:

> "Man longs even for the sake of his mere thinking for a **Thou** corresponding to the I. The conception appears to him to reach its definiteness and certainty only when it reflects from another power of thought. . . . But the objectivity appears in a still more complete form if this separation does not go on in the subject alone, if he really sees the thought outside himself; and this is possible only in another being, representing and thinking like himself." (BMM 27)

and Ludwig Feuerbach, who wrote in 1843,

> "True dialectic is not a monologue of the solitary thinker with himself, it is a dialogue between **I** and **Thou**." (Quoted at BMM 27)

Buber warns that even the notions of Humboldt and Feuerbach do not go far enough. A further step is needed, he claims, in that the Thou cannot be merely ready to receive, and disposed to philosophize along with the I. Rather, the Thou must be viewed as someone who "thinks other things in an other way." (BMM 27) The Other must not be framed by thought, and therefore unreal. The Other must hold his own, even with the **bodily** fact of otherness.

Dialogue is experienced most intimately in the act of love. In contradistinction to the sadomasochistic postures of so many "erotic persons" (so well described by Sartre, and acknowledged by Buber to exist in countless varieties), those who are loyal to the Eros of dialogue experience their partners' life in "simple presence," not as an object that is seen and touched, but rather from the "inner" to the "outer." Partners in dialogue, Buber says "receive the common event from the other's side as well, that is, they receive it from the two sides, and thus for the first time understand in a bodily way what an event is." (BMM 29)

Just as "Dialogue" is helpful for the comprehension of *I and Thou*, the essays "Distance and Relation" and "Elements of the Interhuman" are requisite for a grasp of Buber's philosophical anthropology (which, in turn, elucidates the entire work of the author). The examination of these two essays, it is hoped, will make clear the relation between Buber's ontology and his anthropology.

Distance and Relation

Buber began writing his philosophical anthropology when he was seventy-three years old, and completed it when he was eighty-five. His aim was to answer the question: what is man in his *wholeness*? Philosophy, he said, cannot, through its individual disciplines, answer this question. In every discipline the achievements depend largely on the objectification, on the dehumanization, of a person. Science cannot answer the question either, for it investigates man in selective abstraction from the natural world in which he lives. The inevitable difference between observers is negated, reducing the I as much as possible to an abstract knowing subject. The object of investigation, on the other hand, must be passive and permit categorization.

Buber's writings on I and Thou are for the most part phenomenological descriptions throughout which the author intersperses aphorisms and extended metaphors. His essays on philosophical anthropology aim at providing an *ontological* basis for his philosophy in general. It is here that he addresses the question of the Between (*Dazwischen*) and develops the notions of *distance* and *relation*. When, in *I and Thou*, he states that the I-Thou relation precedes the I-It relation in the infant and in primitive people he means by this statement that these relations emerge in this chronological order, as it were. In the essay "<u>Distance and Relation</u>," (KM 59-71) Buber notes that "setting at a distance" precedes "entering into relation." Here, however, the focus is not on when in the history of the individual or of the group a person becomes a person, but rather, the aim is to explain what in the ontology of man distinguishes him as such, once he is a man.

The principle of human life, Buber says, is built up of a twofold movement such that the one movement is the presupposition of the other. The first, which the author calls "the primal setting at a distance" presupposes the second, "entering into relation," but it should be emphasized that since relation is neither temporal nor spatial, neither can the distancing be so.

"Entering into relation" can be accomplished only with being which has been set at a distance, which has become an "independent opposite." Since only for man does an independent opposite exist, other creatures are not capable of entering into relation. The animal's environment (<u>Umwelt</u>), as conditioned by circumstances which affect the particular species, is the animal's world. An animal perceives only the things which concern it--and it is those things, Buber notes, which make up the world. But would it not be more precise to call it a "realm"? Even the "world of the senses" is a world because it comprises what is perceived and what <u>can be</u> perceived. The animal's organism determines for it the selection from a nature, which, as such, is totally unknown and unknowable to it. Man is the creature (<u>Wesen</u>), according to Buber, through

> whose being (<u>Sein</u>) 'what is' (<u>das Seiende</u>) becomes detached from him, and recognized for itself. It is only the realm which is removed, lifted out from sheer presence, withdrawn from the operation of needs and wants, set at a distance and thereby given over to itself, which is more and other than

a realm. Only when a structure of being is independently over against a living being (<u>Seiende</u>), an independent opposite, does a world exist. (KM 61)

The second movement, entering into relation, is conditioned by the first in that one cannot "think of an existence over against a world which is not also an attitude of relation." (KM 62) This act of entering into relation may be characterized, Buber suggests, as synthesizing apperception, i.e., the apperception of a being as a whole and as a unity. This is achieved not merely by setting at a distance and entering into relation (for that would yield only an aggregate of qualities that can be added to at will) but rather by viewing the "over against" in the world in its <u>full presence</u>, with which a person sets himself, present in his <u>whole person</u>, in relation. Only in such an opposition, says Buber, ". . .are the realm of man and what completes it in spirit, finally one." (KM 63)

Philip Wheelwright has written that Buber's notion parallels that of Renouvier who, "working along neo-Kantian lines supplied personhood (<u>personnalité</u>) as the highest and fullest category that man can grasp."[14] He notes that Buber's inquiry takes a significant step beyond the analysis of Renouvier, and concludes,

> Thus the basic otherness of the objects of human experience is the result of a process of distancing on man's part, but the process is primordial and pre-conscious, and consequently the otherness is (to employ Kantian language) transcendental, not empirical--an essential part of man's transcendental unity of apperception.

Indeed, Buber's ideas on the subject of personhood go beyond the notions of Renouvier and Kant. What Wheelwright fails to notice is the similarity between Buber's "distance and relation" and Hegel's and Sartre's explanations of the internal relation insofar as interhuman relations are concerned. When Wheelwright, in criticizing Buber, asks whether most people, "must we not admit" (sic), do not wish to live so predominantly in the realm of the "between," he shows that he missed one point completely, namely, that choosing to draw back (reflex) from the "between" is one of the basic movements which Buber had described in a masterly way.

Every person needs to be 'confirmed' as what he is, even as what he can become, by the Other. And every person has an innate capacity to confirm his fellow person in this way. Buber notes, "That this capacity lies so immeasurably fallow, constitutes the real weakness and questionableness of the human race." (KM 68) The notion of confirmation has been adopted by a number of psychotherapists who emphasize its importance for a person's 'self-image', and who point to a lack of confirmation in one's present circumstances, or even more important, during one's early years, as the cause of various psychological disorders.

Confirmation is achieved in an event which Buber characterizes as "making present," which rests on a capacity which is possessed by all persons to some extent, namely, "imagining the real." This capacity enables man to grasp a reality arising at a particular moment but not able to be experienced directly. Thus one "imagines" what an Other is wishing, feeling, thinking in *his* *own* *reality*. The ontological significance of "making present," then, lies in the realization of all men that they are set at a distance, that they are made independent by the Other. Buber explains,

> Our fellow men, it is true, live around about us as components of the independent world over against us, but insofar as we grasp each one as a human being he ceases to be a component and is there in his self-being as I am; his being at a distance does not exist merely for me, but it cannot be separated

from the fact of my being at a distance for him. . . .Relation is fulfilled in a full making present when I think of the other not merely as this very one, but experience in the particular approximation of the given moment, the experience of belonging to him as this very one. (KM 70-71)

An animal does not need to be confirmed. It is what it is and never questions its being. Man is different. He belongs to a solitary category. He is surrounded by uncanny forces which often terrify him. But he can find comfort, Buber writes, as "secretly and bashfully he watches for a yes which allows him to person to another. It is from one man to another that the heavenly bread of self-being is passed." (KM 71)

Elements of the Interhuman

Corresponding to Sartre's analysis of groups in *Critique de la raison dialectique* is Buber's essay which addresses the same topic. Moreover, Buber's view is surprisingly similar to Sartre's, on several important points. Both writers agree, for example, that it takes more than a collectivity of persons to form a cohesive group. A group, even if it be cohesive, does not necessarily afford each member within it a personal relation with the other members—although some contacts do arise which favor such relations. The chief characteristic of groups as they have evolved in modern history, however, has been the suppression of the personal element in favor of the purely collective. As a result, individuals are swept into the group and lifted out of their solitude. They need fear the world no longer. The categories and terminology of Sartre are evidently not exactly the same as Buber's. Nevertheless, their views on this subject are as much in agreement as on any other subject. The major difference is that Buber goes beyond the concept of the "group-in fusion" which Sartre seems to consider to be the ideal.

Buber makes a distinction between the "social" and "interhuman." The "social" includes I-It relations as well as I-Thou relations. Most interpersonal relations, in fact, are a mixture of the two. Buber insists that the "interhuman" is a separate dimension; it is the sphere of the "between" of dialogue. That which occurs within the psyche of an individual, the psychological, is only the accompaniment to the dialogue. 'Community', he says, "is the being no longer side by side but *with* one another of a multitude of persons. And this multitude, though it also moves towards one goal, yet experiences everywhere a turning to, a dynamic facing of, the other, a flowing from *I* to *Thou*."[15]

The interhuman is the I-Thou relationship which characterizes dialogue between persons. Since persons can enter into I-Thou relationships with nature and with art as well, the interhuman cannot be synonymous with the dialogical. The confusion which arose from *I and Thou* on this subject is cleared up in the essay "Elements of the Interhuman." I-Thou relationships with things in nature are, and are not, rejected (although Buber admitted that if he were to write *I and Thou* again, he would have sought different categories for such relations)--for man has in common with these things the ability to become an object of observation. And I can address a Thou, be it the Other, or a thing in nature or art, without the Other, or the thing, being able to reciprocate. It is the privilege of man only, however, to impose an insurmountable limit to objectification. Only as a partner can man's being be perceived in its wholeness.

Central to Buber's anthropology is the duality of "being" and "seeming." Basically, the person in whom "being" predominates *is* spontaneous, authentic, real. The "seeming" person is concerned with the image he *projects*--he does not wish his true self to be perceived; therefore he affects an image which is calculated to *appear* spontaneous, authentic, or real. No one is entirely independent of the impression he or she makes on an Other, any more than there could be someone exclusively determined by the impression he or she made. Rather, Buber wishes to distinguish between persons in whose essential attitude "being" or "seeming" predominates. In Buber's view, whatever the meaning of the word 'truth' may be in other realms, it means, in the interhuman realm, that persons communicate themselves as what they _are_ to one another. _Seeming_ offers itself as a help or ruse in a person's attempt to obtain confirmation by the Other, and confirmation, the author has made clear, is indeed essential for a person's self-image. But to yield to seeming, he warns, is a person's essential cowardice; to resist it is his essential courage. Confirmation of what one is, when one _is_ _not_ what he has made himself appear to be, is not really confirmation at all. The subtlety of Buber's insights in this area has been invaluable to psychotherapists such as Carl R. Rogers and Leslie Farber.

Buber has noted that there are three causes which impede the growth of dialogical relations among men. The first was the invasion of "seeming." The second cause is man's inadequacy of perception, his inability, so often, to "imagine the real." The third, and by far the most dangerous, he says, is the manner in which persons attempt to influence the thinking of others. For purposes of illustration, and with elaboration to which only the allusion can be made here, Buber cites as the two basic ways of affecting an Other's views and attitude to life: (1) the imposition of oneself, one's opinions and attitude in a manner which causes the Other to feel that the psychical result of the action was _his_ _own_ _insight_, which has only been liberated by the influence. This way has been perfected in the realm of propaganda. (2) The search and attempt to further in the Other's soul the disposition toward what one has recognized in oneself as right. Since it is right, it is likely to be alive in the microcosm of the Other, at least as a possibility. This second way, Buber states, has been most powerfully developed in the realm of education.

Alluding to Kant's formulation of the Categorical Imperative which enjoins man never to think of and treat an Other only as a means but always at the same time as an independent end, Buber suggest that his own view is essentially close to Kant's. But whereas the latter's principle is expressed as an "ought" sustained by the idea of human dignity, Buber is concerned with the presuppositions of the interpersonal. It is not in isolation that man exists. Individuation, he says, is "the indispensable personal stamp of all realization of human existence. The self as such is not ultimately the essential, but the meaning of human existence given in creation again and again fulfills itself as self." (KM 84-85) Therefore, for the proper existence of the interpersonal *it is necessary* that semblance not intervene to spoil the dialogue, that each person "means" and makes present the Other, and that neither attempts to impose himself on the Other.

In genuine dialogue, each person must make the contribution of his spirit "without reduction and without shiftinghis ground." (KM 85) He must be willing to say what is really in his mind about the subject of the discussion. What one has to say, according to Buber, "at any one time already has the character of something that wishes to be uttered," (KM 86) and it must not be held back. This must not be confused with "unreserved speech," for everything depends on the legitimacy of "what has to be said." Buber's comments on dialogue, which he considers in its genuine form to be an ontological sphere constituted by the authenticity of being, especially when they refer to 'authentic speech' are surprisingly in harmony with those of Heidegger.

The area of Buber's work which is perhaps least compatible with Heidegger's account, or Sartre's, is the ethical philosophy. As will be shown in the section which follows, the reason for this is grounded in the divergent vantage point from which ethics was addressed by these writers. Moreover, since the ontology of Buber is being examined through the study of his divers writing on other topics, his moral philosophy can certainly not be ignored. There is still another compelling reason to include at this point an account of Buber's moral philosophy. Since Sartre never wrote anything referring to Buber, and since the latter refuted Sartre most forcefully in his criticism of Sartre's views on ethics and religion, these arguments are particularly significant in comparing the two writers.

Ethics and Religion

Buber did not write extensively on ethics, nor was he recognized particularly for this phase of his writing. As a matter of fact, it is difficult to separate his ethical philosophy from his theological beliefs. Still he wrote one book, Good and Evil,[16] and a number of essays[17] which address ethical theory. Moreover, his philosophical anthropology especially, but, indeed, almost his entire work, makes allusions to a moral viewpoint which bears his distinctive stamp.

Buber's ethics stresses above everything else the intrinsic value or disvalue (in contrast to the usefulness or harmfulness) of human conduct. The influence of Kant is clearly visible in the ethical writings of the Jewish philosopher, although Buber states that in addition to a criterion of moral "autonomy," other criteria, traditional or perceived by the individual himself, may be involved in deciding what is right and what is wrong in one's own situation. The important thing, Buber says, is that

> the critical flame shoot up ever again out of the depths, first illuminating, then burning and purifying. The truest source of this is a fundamental awareness inherent in all men, though in most varied strengths and degrees of consciousness, and for the most part stifled by them. It is the individual's awareness of what he is "in truth," of what in his unique and non-repeatable created existence he is intended to be.[18]

According to Buber, the religious forms the basis of the ethical. When and to the extent that a person, as a **whole** being, enters and remains in relation to the Absolute, that person, according to Buber, is religious in the strict sense. He explains,

> This presupposes the existence of a Being who, though in himself unlimited and unconditioned, lets other beings, limited and conditioned indeed, exist outside Himself. He even allows them to enter into a relation with him such as seemingly can only exist between limited and conditioned beings. Thus, in my definition of the religious "the Absolute" does not mean something that the human person holds it to be, without anything being said about its existence, but the absolute reality itself, whatever the form in which it presents itself to the human person at this moment.[19]

For Buber, God is immanent as well as transcendent. The absolute can reduce itself to the personal. In this respect, Buber contends "one may understand the personality of God as his act."[20] If a person means by his concept of God all that is, and includes himself therein, he cannot enter into relation and therefore cannot be considered religious in the strict sense. Similarly, if God is to be a person's own self, no matter how complicated the disguises in the "Pseudo-mystical chamber of ghosts and mirrors," the concept of God in this instance will have nothing to do with the real relation.

Buber warns that it is not from the teachings of ethics and religion that one can derive the relation between the two. This can be achieved only by penetrating the concrete, personal situation within each sphere. He notes that the religious person will have a strong tendency to be ethical. On the other hand, the man who seeks distinction and decision in his own soul cannot draw from it, from his soul, absoluteness for his scale of values . . . always it is the religious which bestows, the ethical which receives.[21]

Sartre's comments about religion (e.g., his repeated assertions that God does not exist, that God "spoke to us and is now silent, all that we touch now is his corpse")[22] were considered by Buber to betray a shallow understanding of theology. Choosing to ignore what Sartre really meant by the idea that God once spoke to man but now is silent, namely, that man no longer believes as he did in earlier times, that he can hear God, Buber focused on an issue which contemporary theologians had been arguing. Nietzsche's cry "God is dead!" refers to a God who is immanent, who is no more than an idea in the mind of man and therefore can cease to be useful when man's idea has understands it, "the living God is not only a self-revealing but also a self-concealing God."

Sartre assumed that the problem which tormented Nietzsche, Heidegger and Jaspers, i.e., the combination of the perseverance of the religious need in modern man with the silence of the transcendent, called for renewed courage on the part of existentialists. It must "forget" God, give up once and for all the search of God.[23] He declared that there is no universe which the for-itself does not bring into being and it was this view which Buber found objectionable.

Existence, according to Buber, does not mean "existing for 'oneself', encapsulated in one's own subjectivity." It means, rather, he wrote, "standing <u>over against</u> the x; not an x for which a certain quantity could be substituted, but rather the x itself, the undefinable, the unfathomable."[24] Sartre contends that man does not need God since the Other, any "other" will do just as well.[25] Buber points out that Sartre makes this statement only because for him the Other is an inescapable witness, he who "looks" at me, and if God is to be construed as a witness who also "looks at me," then obviously any Other will suffice. But, Buber asks,

> What if God is not the quintessence of the Other, but rather its absoluteness? And what if it is not primarily the reciprocal relation of subject and object which exists between me and the Other, but rather the reciprocal relation of I and Thou? Each empirical Other does not, of course, remain my Thou, he becomes an It, an object for me, as I for him. It is not so, however, with that absolute Other, the absolute over against me, that undefinable X I call "God."[26]

The author goes on to explain that God can never become an object for him. Rather, the only relation possible is that between an I and the Eternal Thou. Should God choose to remain silent, and in so doing make it impossible for man to attain this relation, it would not be in human subjectivity that the event had occured, but rather in Being itself. Instead of explaining such an "eclipse of God" in sensational terms like "God is dead," Buber suggests that man would do better to "move existentially towards a new happening" through which the dialogue between heaven and earth will be reestablished. Sartre objects to the "religious need" of man. Buber points to it as indicating man's awareness of the silence of the transcendent. Is it productive to speculate on the reason for God's silence? Perhaps so, according to Buber. Unlike Sartre, who points to the silence as reason for man to "recover for himself the creative freedom which he ascribed to God,"[27] Buber suggests that man might continually examine his role, i.e., the part that his hearing or not hearing has played in that silence.

Buber is critical of Sartre's view that the universe exists through man and that therefore man should affirm himself, rather than God, as the being responsible for it. This view, reminiscent of Feuerbach, Buber says, overlooks the fact that the world

> is indeed the composite work of a thousand generations, but it has come into being through the fact that manifold being, which is not our work, meets us, who are, likewise, together with our subjectivity, not our work, . . . All that being is established, we are established, our meeting with it is established, and in this way, the becoming of a world, which takes place through us, is established.[28]

Buber would have man recognize that "creative freedom" is granted to him. Moreover, man should use this freedom properly, i.e., he should construe it as a mission. Human existence, according to Buber means "being sent and being commissioned." Sartre's theory urges mankind to "draw the consequences" from the fact that no unconditioned being speaks to it. The consequences are that there is no universal morality telling us what to do, and so there is no possibility of discovering absolute values. Therefore, Sartre claimed, "all is permitted" to man. Echoing Nietzsche, Sartre declared that if God has been done away with, someone is needed to invent values. "Life has no meaning *a priori*," he said, ". . . it is up to you to give it meaning, and value is nothing else than this meaning which you choose."[29]

The above quotation was taken up by Buber and rejected vehemently.

> One can believe in and accept a meaning, one can set it as a guiding light over one's life if one has discovered it, and not if one has invented it. It can be for me an illuminating meaning, a direction-giving value only if it

has been revealed to me in my meeting with Being, not if I have freely chosen it from among the existing possibilities and perhaps have in addition decided with some fellow creatures: This shall be valid from now on.[30]

It is evident that one cannot isolate Buber's ethics from his religious views. Every topic, in one way or another, is related by the author to its connection with the absolute. Thus, conscience, defined as the voice one hears which urges a person to fulfill what being had intended him to be, ultimately encompasses the response which a person makes. From the response, depending on the degree of "authenticity" (for a person may be mistaken in what he heard and in what he judges to be the appropriate response) the categories of right and wrong can be derived. Guilt results from the realization that one's response to a particular moment was not what it should have been. But ethical decision is more that the responses to a specific situation, it is the stance toward being, of fulfilling one's "mission" in life with respect to one's relationship with God.

Buber's notion of responsibility can be likened, to some extent, to Sartre's "inventing" values after all. If a person is to assess each situation and respond to it according to his own conscience, is he not <u>creating</u> the value of the moral act? Buber would oppose such a comparison. First, he would reiterate that the value was discovered, not invented. But more importantly, perhaps, he would insist that the ground of the ethical discussion be shifted from the universal to the concrete, from the past or future to the present, from the It to the Thou. Besides, he wrote,

> No responsible person remains a stranger to norms. But the command inherent in a genuine norm never becomes a maxim and the fulfillment of it never a habit. . . . Even the most universal norm will at times be

>   recognized only in a very special situation.
>   (BMM 114)

making unmistakably clear that values are revealed and discovered, in concrete situations. To the extent that a man is capable of saying Thou, of responding authentically with his whole being, his moral act will be good, or right. Conversely there is "never a wholeness where downtrodden appetites lurk in the corner."[31] Where a person's wholeness is not brought into being, where one fails to unify his scattered passions and mobilize them into the service of the unique direction which must be taken, there, the action taken is wrong.

Buber explains evil as occurring in two stages. The first of these is the failure to respond with one's whole being (good can only be done with the whole soul, according to Buber, whereas evil can never be done with the whole soul). The first stage is often the cause of guilt feeling. Man becomes aware, sooner or later, through the consequence of his act or else through a better understanding of his intention in performing it, that it was the "wrong" thing to do. The second stage of evil is the actual decision to do that which a person has already determined in his soul to be the wrong act. Thus the first stage of evil results from indecision, lack of direction; one "slides" into it. The second stage is reached through deliberate decision. Time and again, man has the freedom to choose between good and evil. The "evil" man need but to act with his whole soul, decisively, and respond to the demand of the moment in a dialogical way and he will cease to be evil. Should he choose repeatedly to do that which is wrong, he may lose the ability to confirm himself (in which case, more than ever, confirmation by an Other is of utmost necessity) as the self with which the person identifies, and he may then fall into a pathological crisis of identity.[32] Maurice Friedman notes that there is a close relation between Buber's tendency to ascribe reality to evil and tragic events like the

Holocaust and the war in Palestine. He quotes Buber as saying:

> It is significant that it is in our times that the man has arisen in whom the tension between what one is and what one should be is dissolved--the man without conscience. The secret of Hitler's effectiveness lies, in fact, in his complete and fundamental absence of restraint.[33]

At this point it is important to return to Buber's philosophical anthropology and expand on the perspective which he presents on the relative merits of other writers on this area of thought. It may not be readily apparent how an examination of the author's philosophical anthropology bears on the central topic of the present study. However, there is much insight to be gained from any part of Buber's work which addresses the notions of other philosophers, especially in regard to personality. It is anticipated that the self, the Other, the "essential We," indeed, the entire work of Buber, will be grasped with more clarity than otherwise, as a result of the analysis which follows.

Philosophical Anthropology

Buber claims that at times when man has felt himself solitary he has been most disposed to self-reflection and best suited for it. During epochs which he calls 'epochs of habitation' (in contrast to the solitary times which are designated 'epochs of homelessness') he is not inclined to raise the anthropological question, _What is man_? In his appropriately titled essay,[34] providing little elaboration, but rather sketching the history of philosophical anthropology to suit his images, Buber skips from one philosopher to the next. As noted at the beginning of this chapter on Buber, the notions of this author regarding ontology, particularly the self and the Other, must be gleaned from his divers writings. In tracing the history of man's attempt to answer the anthropological question, or his failure to even raise it, Buber does pause, when a closer examination is essential, to explain his views of the subject. Therefore, his comments regarding anthropology are indeed an important source of information about his ontology. His analysis of Hegel and Marx is perhaps more sketchy than one might expect, and that of Feuerbach and Nietzsche is also limited. Buber is at his best in the second part of the essay, where his critique of Heidegger and Scheler is extended; this text is invaluable in presenting the author's own theory.

Berhard Geroethuysen said of Aristotle that with him man is comprehended only in the world, Buber notes, but the world is not comprehended in man (BMM 126). Aristotle's geocentric spherical system is the perfection of the tendency to place man in his fixed space in the world which itself is a self-contained space. The *visual* image of the universe of *things*, and now man is a thing amoung these things, objectively comprehensible as one species beside other species.

When the spherical and unified world of Aristotle collapsed, when man could no longer grasp as truth anything but a world which was divided against itself, out of his solitude Augustine posed the anthropological question once again: What is man in his wholeness? In Manichaeism, man does not have a fixed place in the world. Comprising soul and body, he is at the same time the *scene* of the struggle and the *prize*. Having found salvation in Christianity as a salvation which has already occurred, Augustine asks, "What is man that thou are mindful of him?" With this question, the *grande profundum*, the great mystery which is man, is raised once again, and it affects all future philosophy.

As Christianity provided a new "habitation" for the post-Augustinian west, once again there was a self-enclosed universe. Aquinas saw no special problem with man as man such as Augustine had experienced. To be sure, in Aquinas's system man is a species of a special kind since in him the soul which is the lowest of the spirits, is united with the human body, which is the highest of physical things. But the anthropological question, according to Buber, has come to a rest again in this epoch.

In Carolus Bovillus and in Cusa there had already emerged a new questioning about man as man. The finite world still provided a "home" for man, but it appears, increasingly more clearly, that man *can know*. Bovillus excepts God, but otherwise he and the other thinkers of the Renaissance assume that man can know all, can comprehend the entire universe, having been created outside of it as its spectator. Cusa spoke of the spatial and temporal infinity of the universe, thus destroying the medieval pattern, but this infinity is perceived only intellectually--not existentially. It was not until Copernicus destroyed the house, to use Buber's metaphor, that man became no longer secure.

Pascal's anguish expressed in "*le silence éternel de ces espaces infinis m'effraie*," reflects a new homelessness. Man's place in the cosmos, between the two infinities, is made more precise than ever before. Man's relation to nature is such that he can be killed by a vapor, by a drop of water. But in dying man would know what had killed him, and nature would not. What is decisive is not that a person dares to confront the universe and know it, but that he knows the relation between the universe and himself. Man once again has his own problematic. Spinoza attempted to master the situation. Man must accept his homelessness, he seemed to be saying, but, no matter. The important thing is that man devote himself to *natura naturans*, so that he may be lifted "above the mere outline character of his *natura naturata*, which is drawn into the system only conceptually, as the aggregate of the divine modes, and in which the kinds and order of being are not really grasped and united" (BMM 134). A person does not *need* a universe, he needs to understand that God loves himself in *him*. If man could understand

Spinoza's point of view, and accept it unreservedly, he would no longer be problematic to himself.

In Buber's account, Kant was the first to understand the anthropological question in such a way that an answer could be given to Pascal's concern.[35] The answer was not directed metaphysically; but epistemologically it grasped the problems: "what sort of a world is it, which man knows? How can man, as he is, in his altered reality, know it all? How does man stand in the world he knows in this way--what is it to him and what is he to it?" (BMM 135). The answers to those questions refer man back to himself. It is the mystery of a person's own comprehension of the world and of his own being that appears to him hostile and terrifying. *What is man* is thus shown to be a genuine question which, Buber says, is "shown in all clarity as a legacy to our age" (BMM 137). As noted before, Buber claimed that Kant, having posed the question in all clarity, did not really set about resolving it. Nevertheless the task was set for future generations.

Hegel's system is described as having dispossessed "the concrete human person and the concrete community in favor of universal reason, its dialectical processes and its objective structures" (BMM 135). Thinkers like Kierkegaard and Marx, whose views were quite divergent from Hegel's, nonetheless interpreted human life in terms of a dialectic. Kierkegaard saw it as a movement from the esthetic to the ethical and from there to the religious. Marx considered it to be a movement from primitive communal economy to private property, and from there to socialism. Buber contends that the young Hegel had indeed begun in genuine anthropological fashion to find what he called "the unity of the whole man" (cited in BMM 138) and later strove to create an anthropological metaphysic. But in the later Hegel, even in the entry under "Anthropology" in the *Encyclopedia of the Philosophical Sciences*, the significance and reality of human life are not addressed. Universal reason, not man, is the starting point of Hegel's system. Buber characterizes Hegel's new direction as follows,

> All the contradiction in human life and history does not lead to the anthropological questionableness and question, but presents itself as a "ruse" which the idea makes use of in order to reach its own perfection through the very fact that it overcomes contradiction. The claim is made that Kant's fundamental question, What is man? is finally answered here; in reality it is obscured, even eliminated. (BMM 139)

For Buber, Hegel's system is the third significant attempt to provide security for Western man after Aristotle's cosmological theory and Aquinas's theological doctrine. Hegel's is labeled the 'logological' attempt. Unlike the preceding epochs of habitation, however, which lasted relatively long periods of time, Hegel's system was immediately attacked. The reason for this, Buber speculates, is that an intellectual image of the universe built on time can never provide the same feeling of security as one which builds on space. An image which incorporates "the goal of universal history" cannot give assurance. Cosmological time is not actual human time but a time conceived in thought. Therefore, the logological attempt was soon to be superseded by the present epoch, which Buber considers to be the most homeless of all ages.

Buber admits that there was an important phenomenon within the sphere of influence of the Hegelian system, which was not marked by negative criticism of it. This phenomenon, Marx's "sociological reduction" of Hegel's method, was meant to substitute an image of society—better yet, an image of how society was to reach its perfection for the no longer necessary image of the universe. Commenting on the effect of Hegel's and Marx's thought, Buber writes,

> Hegel as it were compulsorily combined the course of the stars and of history into a speculative security. Marx, who confined himself to the human world, ascribed to it

alone a security in regard to the future, which is likewise dialectic, but has the effect of an actual security. Today this security has perished in the ordered chaos of a terrible historical revulsion. Gone is the calm, a new anthropological dread has arisen, the question about man's being faces us as never before in all its grandeur and terror--no longer in philosophical attire, but in the nakedness of existence. (BMM 145)

Kant, in opposition to rationalism, and following Hume, had made cognition the paramount philosophical problem. Hegel insisted that no immediate object should be placed at the beginning of philosophy, but rather, he claimed, philosophical thinking must "anticipate." If anything were to be the beginning of phisosophy, it would be "pure being" which Hegel explained as "pure abstraction" (cited in BMM 146). On this basis the object of philosophy was to be 'universal reason', not human cognition. Feuerbach opposed both Kant and Hegel. In his **Principles of the Philosophy of the Future**, he wrote that the principle of the new philosophy was to be man's **real, whole** being.[36]

Buber's objection to Feuerbach's ideas was noted in the "Historical Background" section of the present work. His criticism was focused on Feuerbach's reduction of anthropology which leads to **unproblematic** man rather than to man, say, as Pascal viewed him. Even more misguided, according to Buber, is the notion that individual man for himself does not have man's being in himself. It is in community, in the unity of man with man, that man's being is significantly contained, according to Feuerbach. Buber credits Feuerbach with the discovery of the Thou, but he does not agree with the notion that individual man is unambiguous, any more than that in the individual person being is not significantly contained. Buber's essay, "The Question to the Single One" (BMM 40-82), primarily a critique of Kierkegaard and Max Stirner on this subject, makes clear the author's view on the dangers of collectivity which entangle man in a manifold We.

Nietzsche brought man back into the center of his philosophising about the universe. Defining him at first as a species not yet established but becoming, in transition, he went on to depict man as an "embryo" of future man. The real man would be the one who has a good conscience toward his will to power. Buber took issue with the sociological and anthropological presuppositions about the history of the origins of man. Moreover, the psychological and historical view of the will to power was also found to be erroneous. Greatness includes power, Buber said, but not a will to power. Power means the capacity to realize what one wishes to realize, but the great man is avid not for this capacity "but for what he wishes to be capable of" (BMM 151).

Although Nietzsche did not give a positive foundation to anthropology, he did point to the questionableness of human life as the most important subject of philosophising. To be sure, his interest lay in the question of how a creature such as man has emerged from the animal world. Augustine, Pascal, and Kant had perceived something in man which could not be explained in terms of nature and its development alone. Before Nietzsche, therefore, man was not merely a species, but a category. As Buber explains, "The problem which Nietzsche neglected, that such a being exists, is only shifted in his view from the realm of the being of a species to the realm of its becoming" (BMM 155). For post-Nietzschean philosophy man became once again not only a species, but a category.

As noted earlier, Buber's evaluation of the contributions made by the various philosophers who addressed philosophical anthropology is subjective. It is so in more ways than one. First, he selects the thinkers who are to be considered, and neglects to mention why others are not. Second, he limits his judgment to that portion of a writer's total work which supports his contention. Third, he employs idiosyncratic criteria for the appraisal of a theory, seldom undertaking to explain why these criteria and not those of the other writer in question are appropriate. The effect of this method of evaluation is forceful. It is doubtful that Buber could achieve comparable results had he been more "scholarly." Certainly, his own position would not have been rendered so clearly. Therefore, one is tempted to accept his critique for what it is worth, i.e., as a statement of what he believes, and of how he perceives the ideas of divers philosophers. However, the first section of Buber's long essay hardly qualifies as a serious attack upon the authors who are mentioned and evaluated.

Such is not the case with Buber's comments on Heidegger and Scheler. In these thinkers, he held, the anthropological problem reached maturity in that the problem of man is treated as an independent philosophical problem. With careful attention to details and patient elaboration, Buber examines those two writers' work, providing not only some valid criticism of their views, but making his own view clear.

The critique of Heidegger begins with the observation that when Augustine, Pascal and Kierkegaard found themselves solitary in a mysterious universe which they could not understand, try as they might, they sought a form of being that is not included in the world, a divine form of being with whom they might communicate. In Nietzsche, the solitariness was such, and the homelessness of the epoch had become so cold and strict, that the philosopher could not reach out to meet a divine form. This was the basis of Nietzsche's cry that God is dead. Thereafter, man could turn only to himself. The mystery of the being of man was replaced by Heidegger with the questions of fundamental ontology, i.e., existence in its relation to its own being.[37]

Heidegger's theory isolates from the wholeness of life the realm in which man is related to himself, Buber notes. Not only is a divine being not considered, the Other is ignored, too. From the absolutized, "temporally conditioned situation of the radically solitary man" (BMM 168), Heidegger attempts to derive the essence of human existence. According to Buber, this is like trying to derive it from a nightmare--in which a person can no longer say "Thou" to the "dead" divine form and, perhaps worse, he cannot even say "thou" to another living man. Besides, the notion of "self-being" of the man of "real" existence, contradicts Heidegger's own statement that man's being is by nature *in the world*, in which he is surrounded by things and other men with whom he coexists. According to Buber, Heidegger understands fully, and even acknowledges, that a relation with the Other is essential. Yet a relation of "solicitude" cannot *as such* be an essential relation. Instead of setting one person's life in direct relation with the Other's, Buber says, it juxtaposes one person's solicitous help with another person's lack and need of it.

Solicitude may lead to a fuller, more dialogic relationship. What begins as pity, compassion, care for an Other, may blossom into a relation of reciprocity. But in *mere* solicitude, Buber admonishes, a persons remains essentially within himself--he is concerned with the other, but he is not anxious that the Other be concerned with him. In an essential relation, Buber says,

> . . . the other becomes present not merely in the imagination or feeling, but in the depths of one's substance, so that one experiences the mystery of the other being in the mystery of one's own. The two participate in one another's lives in very fact, not psychically, but ontically. (BMM 170)

Buber's criticism of Heidegger is severe on this point. If self-being is to be *the* ultimate of which

145

existence is capable, the insight of Feuerbach that the essence of man is not contained in himself but in the unity of man with man seems to be ignored. For Heidegger, the essence of man is in himself--all he need do in order to bring it to existence is to become a "resolved" self. Therefore, Buber notes, Heidegger's self is a closed system. Kierkegaard's 'individual' is an open system. It is the presupposition to entering into relationship with God. If man must renounce the essential relation to an Other (as Kierkegaard himself chose to do with his fiancée) in order to enter into relation with the absolute, he does so fully cognizant of the essential relation he is renouncing. There is a Thou uttered with the whole being, to the Other, (even if only to tell him/her why the essential relation must be renounced). In Heidegger's system there is no "Thou." "One does not say this Thou to the man for whom one is merely solicitous" (BMM 172), Buber remarks.

Another notion which Heidegger is accused of having derived from Kierkegaard, but in adapting it to cohere with "fundamental ontology" has transformed so that it has lost its true significance, is the concept of das Man, "one." In the account of both writers-- and Buber also is in agreement on this point--it is necessary in order to reach self-being to disengage oneself from the crowd, the faceless and nameless mass which reduces everything and everyone to a uniform flatness. But again, self-being for Kierkegaard is an essential step on one's way to the absolute, whereas for Heidegger it is an end in itself. Besides, according to Buber, there is on the level of the multitude of men a category which corresponds to the essential Thou, namely, the essential We.

In contrast to Sartre who, as indicated above, categorized neatly the types of groups (e.g., the group-in-series, the group-in-fusion) which characterize human society, Buber makes a distinction, within every possible group, between those members of a group who stand in essential relation to an Other and those who do not. 'We' can be applied only to a community of independent, self-responsible persons within which an ontic directness is the presupposition of the I-Thou relation. "The *We*," Buber notes, "includes the *Thou* potentially. Only men who are capable of truly saying *Thou* to one another can truly say *We* with one another (BMM 176).

The "essential *We*" has been little recognized, according to Buber. Most groups are considered in respect to their goals and not their inner structure. To be sure, there are transient forms of the essential *We*. Buber's descriptions of these closely resemble those of Sartre in depicting groups-in-fusion. Buber points to such groups as the only realm where a person can be saved from the "one." It is not by separation from the crowd but by being bound up in genuine communion that a man is truly saved.

Buber is more sympathetic toward Scheler than he is toward Heidegger. He agrees with neither thinker, insisting that both have failed to grasp the essential relations (between man and things in the world, man and man, man and God) which distinguish man as man. Heidegger's metaphysic, as Buber understands it, precludes any relation except that between *Dasein* and its own being. Scheler did not address the category of the Between, but at least he realized that one cannot abstract from the concreteness of man his own existence, his relation to himself. Instead, Scheler was eager to study man in connection with other creatures what does he have in common with them, and how does he differ from them?

Deeply influenced by Hegel and Nietzsche, the anthropology of Scheler reflects an overestimation of the significance of time for the absolute, according to Buber. God *is* not, he *becomes*, he *is in time*, in Scheler's metaphysic--which determines his anthropology. This notion had been espoused by Buber in his youth, when he had been under the influence of German mysticism, from Meister Eckhart to Angelus Silesius, and later the Kabbala and Hasidism, but he abandoned this view in his later writings.

This is not the place to examine in detail Buber's criticism of Scheler's ideas of 'spirit' and 'impulse' as the ground of primal being. The numerous ramifications of such an examination would not provide sufficient insight into Buber's ontology to warrant such a digression, and to do justice to the criticism one would need to digress at length. Nor is it essential that Buber's comments regarding Scheler's view on what distinguishes man significantly from other living creatures be reported at this point. Perhaps the most important element of Buber's commentary about Scheler, indeed of his entire anthropological work, is his detailed account of the sphere of the Between which he proposes as the proper starting point of any anthropology.

The thought of our epoch, in Buber's view, is preoccupied with "individualism or collectivism," yet the fundamental aspect of human existence is neither individual, as such, nor the aggregate, as such. Each, he says,

> . . . considered by itself, is a mighty abstraction. The individual is a fact of existence in so far as he steps into a living relation with other individuals. The aggregate is a fact of existence in so far as it is built up of living units of relation. The fundamental fact of human existence is man with man. What is peculiarly characteristic of the human world is above all that something takes place between one being and another the like of which can be found nowhere in nature. (BMM 203)

Buber's anthropology is not comprehensive. His analysis of art, kinship systems, language, history, etc., is limited to the observations and conclusions which support his ontological understanding of human life. Indeed, it may be that only in a metaphoric sense does the designation of 'philosophical anthropology' apply to his writings in this area, notwithstanding the author's numerous statements of his intention to address this discipline. Be that as it may, the ontological sphere of the Between is more comprehensible, after his anthropology has been reviewed, as are Buber's views on dialogue and his thoughts on philosophy of religion.

In a similar study of his religious writings, i.e., biblical exegesis, explanations of Hasidism and the recounting of Hasidic tales, the extended comparison between Judaism and Christianity,[38] and of his political essays,[39] one could uncover further elucidation of Buber's philosophy. In all his works, except the very early attempts, the same themes are repeated in subtle variations: the notion of dialogue, the emphasis on relation, the tension of unity and diversity, of the Between and polarity, the presence of the Eternal Thou in every relation between persons who address each other as Thou.

Footnotes

1. Martin Buber, *Ich und Du*, *Werke*, vol. I, Schriften zur Philosophie (Munich: Kösel, 1962), The original edition in German appeared in 1923. I have referred to the German text whenever linguistic or conceptual problems indicated the necessity of doing so. Otherwise, for convenience, I have alluded to the English version, *I and Thou*, 2nd ed., trans. Ronald Gregor Smith (New York: Charles Schribner's Sons, 1958). (Hereafter IT).

2. Robert E. Wood, *Martin Buber's Ontology: An Analysis of I and Thou*, (Evanston: Northwestern University Press, 1968).

3. Maurice S. Friedman, *Martin Buber: The Life of Dialogue* (New York: Harper Torchbooks, 1955).

4. Rivka Horwitz, *Buber's Way to I and Thou: An Historical Analysis of the First Publication of Martin Buber's Lectures "Religion als Gegenwart"* (Heidelberg: Verlag Lambert Schneider, 1978).

5. See recently published Williard Moonan's, *Martin Buber: An Annotated Bibliography of Scholarship in English* (New York: Garland Publishing, 1979). A comprehensive bibliography of Buber scholarship in languages other than English is now being compiled by Williard Moonan for the same publisher.

6. Ibid., p. 11.

7. Edmund Husserl, "The crises of European Humanity and Philosophy," *The Search for Being*, ed, and trans. Jean Wilde and William Kimmel (New York: Noonday, 1962, cited in Wood, *Martin Buber's Ontology*, p. XI.

8. Ernst Cassirer, "'Spirit' and 'life' in Contemporary Philosophy," cited in Wood, *Martin Buber's Ontology*, p. XI.

9. Wood, *Martin Buber's Ontology*, p. 39.

10. Grete Schaeder, *The Hebrew Humanism of Martin Buber*, trans. Noah J. Jacobs (Detroit: Wayne State University Press, 1973), p. 151.

11. Rivka Horwitz notes that Buber's lectures, entitled "Religion als Gegenwart," were transcribed faithfully and accurately by a stenographer. These lectures were the raw material for which the author later sought precise expression. Mrs. Horwitz states: "The terminology of the lectures is far less definitive that that of *I and Thou*, which is stronger and more decisive. The word pairs "I-It" and "I-Thou" do not appear in the lectures; Buber instead uses the terms "It-World" and "Thou-World." *Buber's Way to I and Thou*, p. 35.

12. Martin Buber, "The Word that is Spoken," in *The Knowledge of Man*, ed. and trans. Maurice Friedman and Ronald Gregor Smith (New York: Harper & Row, 1965), p.116. (Hereafter *KM*).

13. Eugen Biser, "Martin Buber," *Philosophy Today* VII, no. 2 (1963): 108b.

14. Philip Wheelwright, "Buber's Philosophical Anthropology," *PMB*, p. 82. The allusion to Renouvier refer to Charles Renouvier, *Essais de critique générale: Premier essai* (1854). In the 1912 edition, vol. 2, pp. 177-84.

15. Buber, *BMM*, p. 31. For an extended analysis of Buber's views on social groups and community, see his collection of essays, *Paths in Utopia* (Boston: Beacon Press, 1958), in which the author provides a critical account of the growth of the Utopian ideal from the perspective of Marxist theory, and

also where he illustrates several attempts to realize this ideal, such as the Zionist Kibbutz (of which Buber was the ideological godfather) and the Moshav, ventures in communal socialism which did not founder. In addition, much insight in this area of Buber's thought can be gained from a reading of *Hasidism and Modern Man* (New York: Harper & Row, 1958), in which Buber describes the popular communal mysticism which deeply affected East European Jewry during the eighteenth and nineteenth centuries.

16. Martin Buber, *Good and Evil* (New York: Charles Scribner's Sons, 1952).

17. "Religion and Modern Thinking" and "Religion and Ethics" in *Eclipse of God*, trans. Maurice Friedman, (New York: Harper & Row, 1957), "The Question to the Single One" and "The Education of Character," in *BMM*, and in addition, the hundreds of Hasidic tales retold by Buber which illustrate, in the description and in the consequences of conflict situations, his particular moral viewpoint.

18. Buber, "Religion and Ethics," in *Eclipse of God*, p. 96.

19. Ibid.

20. Ibid., p. 97.

21. Ibid., p. 98.

22. Jean-Paul Sartre, "Un Nouveau Mystique," in *Situations I* (Paris: Gallimard, 1947), p. 153.

23. Ibid., p. 153

24. Buber, *Eclipse of God*, p. 67.

25. Sartre, *Situations*, p. 185

26. Buber, *Eclipse of God*, pp. 67-68.

27. Sartre, in *EN*, *Existentialism*, and in many interviews.

28. Buber, *Eclipse of God*, p. 69.

29. In his essay "Existentialism." In Jean-Paul Sartre, *Existentialism from Dostoevsky to Sartre*, ed. Walter Kaufmann (New York: World Publishing Co., 1956), p. 309.

30. Buber, *Eclipse of God*, p. 70.

31. Buber, *Good and Evil*, p. 129.

32. This description brings to mind the personality types of such psychopaths as Charles Manson, "Son of Sam," and the like.

33. Friedman, *Martin Buber, The Life*, pp. 110-111.

34. Buber, "What is Man?", *BMM*, pp. 118-205. The material which follows is drawn largely from this essay, considered by many commentators to be the culmination of the author's philosophical anthropology.

35. See pp. 16-19 above.

36. See p. 27 above. (Emphasis mine).

37. Nathan Rotenstreich, in Buber's "Dialogical Thought," (PMB, 126-27), suggests that Buber may not be doing justice to one's own being and the relation to an Other. The two relations could be viewed as lying on different levels. The ontological question refers to self-consciousness, whereas the ontic sphere could and does include one's fellow man.

38. See Martin Buber, *Two Types of Faith*, trans,
    Norman Goldhawk (New York: Harper Torchbooks,
    1961).

30. See Martin Buber, *Paths in Utopia*, and *Pointing
    the Way*, trans. Maurice Friedman (New York: Harper
    Torchbooks, 1963).

CHAPTER V

OBSERVATIONS ON BUBER'S POINT OF VIEW

Buber's work has been evaluated favorably by almost all commentators. Credit is given to his originality, his insights, his poetic images, his humanism and, most of all, his convincing insistence on the importance of examining interpersonal relations. His categories of I-Thou and I-It, the analysis of philosophical anthropology, political and religious writings--these have received widespread acceptance and have given impetus to further exploration. But there are aspects of Buber's work which have been attacked by a number of writers. His philosophical writings are not tight, thorough or consistent, some say. Others find him dogmatic, unwilling to consider alternative positions. Like Heidegger, he often makes pronouncements which, having been made, are held to settle the matter at issue. Along with the praise so often given to this writer, there are reservations about his epistemology. It goes without saying that Buber's theology and the philosophical notions derived from it have not been accepted without exception by thinkers who espouse different religious beliefs.

Perhaps the most persistent criticism leveled at Buber's total work is that his insistence on relation as the primary fact of human life is unwarranted. Authentic human existence, according to Kierkegaard, Heidegger and Sartre, need not rely so heavily on the intersubjective element. On the contrary, these writers believe that great efforts must be made to separate the individual from the emotional entanglement in which persons so often lose their own sense of self. Even Buber recognizes, at some points, that the individual is the primary factor in human beings. Nathan Rotenstreich, supporting his contention that Buber is inconsistent on this point, quotes the following statements: "Certainly in order to be able to go to the other, you must have the starting place, you must have been, you must be with yourself" (BMM 21) and "It is true that the child says Thou before it learns to say I, but on the height of personal existence one must truly be able to say I in order to know the mystery of the Thou in its whole truth" (BMM 175).[2] These statements ostensibly point to an inner discrepancy in Buber's system. Rotensteich seems to be demanding to know which comes first, the chicken or the egg. The inconsistency fades away, however, when one recalls that in Buber's ontology the self becomes a self through his relation with an Other. Since human beings interrelate with more than one Other throughout their lives, their character (their facticity, Sartre would say) is shaped by their encounters with other men. As a person enters into relation, therefore, he brings with him the effect of all his prior encounters. If he has been confirmed again and again as the individual he is and wants to be, his identity will be strong, his potential to engage in a dialogical relationship will be enhanced, and it will be his prerogative to do so. On the other hand, the insecure, uncertain, disoriented and dependent individual is more likely, like Alfred J. Prufrock, to be "seeming." He may try to project an image of himself such as the Other will find more desirable, more attractive. On a deeper level, such a person will realize that the self thus accepted and desired by the Other is not his real self.

It is not on the ontological level that Buber speaks of "Beginning with Oneself."[3] Rather, in the ethical dimension, even in the spiritual fulfillment of one's potential, a person is enjoined to look inward. There is no contradiction here. Conflict situations often derive from internal as well as external elements. But Hasidic teaching precludes the isolation of elements from the whole,

> Real transformation, real restoration, at first of the single person and subsequently of the relationship between him and his fellow man, can only be achieved by the comprehension of the whole as a whole. (Putting it paradoxically: the search for the center of gravity shifts it and thereby frustrates the whole attempt at overcoming the problematics involved).[4]

Conflict situations, in Buber's account, although they appear to be between a self and the Other, are often but the results of a conflict situation within the self's own soul. If a person can overcome the inner conflict, he will be able to go out to his fellow men and meet them in new, transformed relationships. Buber notes that men tend to avoid this reversal. They point to the Other, and demand that *he* resolve the inner conflict within his own soul. Thus, when an individual sees himself in contrast with other individuals, and not as a partner in dialogue, he falls into the fundamental error which Hasidism denounces.

There is another issue regarding Buber's theory, not related to the one above, with which Rotenstreich, among others,[5] disagrees. That is, even if it were granted that mutuality of human relations is a kind of entelachy of persons, it does not follow that persons must be defined as creatures of mutuality. One's relation to himself, in terms of soul-searching (to use Buber's phrase), or self-reflection, as was noted above, is an important element of the interpersonal relation. As Rotenstreich puts it, ". . . as the identification of a field of reality presupposes the idea of reality, so the identification of a dialogical situation presupposes the idea of man ascontent..."[6] At this point we are brought back to another criticism often made of Buber, namely, the charge that his metaphysics is confusedly articulated.

Hartshorne, who admits reading his own doctrines into Buber,[7] finds strange the idea of a God who cannot be thought, but can only be addressed. Yet in expressing this idea, one speaks <u>about</u> God, not merely <u>to</u> him. Moreover, an abstract characterization is attributed to God, that of being sensitively relative to each individual. Hartshorne explains,

> To know God who is Thou for you, I must know you in your individual uniqueness, as disclosed to the individual of higher order for whom alone that uniqueness is transparent. Insofar as I know my own intimacy rather than yours, I must know my God rather than yours, and I can know my God only insofar as my self-knowledge goes, in the act of living in the divine presence—a very limited, largely practical sort of awareness which Buber described better than most writers.[8]

The solution in finding a way to discuss the undiscussible, according to Hartshorne, lies in the distinction which must be made between the abstract and the absolute, on the one hand, and the concrete and the relative, on the other. The actual Thou, he notes, cannot be "absolute," for what is required in this case is precisely "relation." However, the general principle of relativity can itself be characterized by absoluteness. There is no alternative to relation as such, Hartshorne makes clear. "That there are relations, some relations or other, is not a relative fact, for to what could it be relative?"[9] On the other hand, Relativity, as an absolute principle, is twofold: the common relativity exemplified by, for example, the interdependence of human beings, and also, according to Hartshorne, the transcendental form of relativity which he calls the divine essence, the divine principle, (which corresponds fairly closely to what Whitehead call the "Consequent Nature" of God). This transcendental Relativity, Hartshorne says, is not God, it is the essence, the principle of God; and the whole discovery of existential theology is that God is superessential: he is actual. Thus Hartshorne proposes a more accurate way of explaining the Eternal Thou. He writes,

> The divine form of relativity, the divine way of addressing and being addressed as Thou is not the actual divine Thou itself, as your God now, or mine. Transcendental relativity is what all possible cases of the divine Thou have in common (or that in which all are similar to one another). It is the highest abstraction, like any abstraction it is It, not Thou.[10]

It is interesting to note that at the end of the volume of *The Philosophy of Martin Buber*, where Buber was given the opportunity to comment on the thirty essays addressed to his work, he did not reply to Hartshorne's ideas. Could it be that the refinements suggested by the latter were acceptable to Buber, or that they are unusually difficult to refute? Probably so, for Buber did not hesitate to point out errors and lack of understanding on the part of many other critics of his thought. Besides, Hartshorne does an excellent job of explicating several of Buber's controversial notions, e.g., the possibility of addressing a tree as Thou, the logical structure of the contrast between I-Thou and I-It, in a manner which renders them tenable to the most skeptical reader. For this, it must be supposed, Buber was appreciative.

As noted, the ethical writings of Buber are numerous and, considering the ethical implications of his philosophical anthropology, theology, etc., it is not surprising to find that commentaries on this aspect of his thought abound. For the most part, they credit him with articulating a fundamental basis for ethics which had hitherto been neglected. Interpersonal relations had indeed been examined by earlier writers, as the first section of this study indicates, but Buber's contribution to a clearer understanding of this field is acknowledged to be substantial. To be sure, there have been many questions raised about his moral philosophy. A review of these questions will certainly be more fruitful than one which would reiterate the praise so often tendered the author.

It must be remembered that in Buber's moral philosophy, values are absolute. In this respect, as in so many others, he was influenced by Kant, who believed that anything less than absolute is not binding. Considerations of interest, fear, etc., have to do with expediency, or with prudence, but not with morality. Values are discovered, Buber said, they are revealed by God. the person who affirms that he is duty-bound to choose a particular course of action affirms that he is bound absolutely.

Buber was well aware that it is often difficult to ascertain whether the ostensible revelation came from God or from one of his many imitators (e.g., the "cause," a false prophet, a delusion). The risk of error in this respect is always a reality. Commenting on Kierkegaard's notion of the "suspension of the ethical," Buber warned that we must be especially cautious if we are bid to do something which departs radically from the prevailing ethical norms (thus Abraham should have been skeptical when he heard the angel directing him to sacrifice his only son, Isaac, in order to prove his faith in God). In our day, more than ever, Buber remarked, "false absolutes rule over the soul, which is no longer able to put them to flight through the image of the true."[11]

Criticism of this stance is predictable. By what criterion can a person distinguish between true and false address? Marvin Fox finds the problem particularly troublesome with regard to "the claims of nations or religious groups who appeal to the superior validity of great moments in their past."[12] And what about the person who desires to be moral but hears claims and counter claims, conflicting voices, Fox asks; how is he to know which voice is that of the absolute, and which mimics the Divine? The problem is further complicated, according to Fox, by Buber's view of revelation (which, in Buber's account, is a "mixture of the divine and the human," in that man conditions what he receives, he "modifies" revelation in his meeting with God). To what extent is the moral agent directed by the address of the Divine, if he has participated in the revelation? Fox raises two questions on this issue, both of which were taken up by Buber in the latter's "Reply to my Critics."[13] The first is why should a man's own modification of revelation be binding on him, and, the second, cannot the modification of revelation in effect be a person's own invention? In response to the first question, Buber explains that in the original sphere of receiving revelation, man does not "modify" through his own action. He cites, as illustration, the revelation received by Moses, which seized him as he was, i.e., the person striving for revelation. Unfortunately, Buber is not sufficiently explicit. He does not elaborate on the idea of the "original sphere of received revelation." As for the second question, alluding to man's participation in revelation as "invention," Buber finds it preposterous to assume that revelation in which God has a share and revelation subjectively "invented: could ever be confused.[14] But again, Buber's language is not precise. The questions raised by Fox appear to point to a problem in Buber's ethics, namely, a vague intuitionism, in that the moral agent, providing that he is in genuine dialogue with God, "knows' what is right and is able to discover values without much danger of error.

There is an important point to be made in regard to Buber's ethics. Although he wrote an essay on the difference between ethics and religion, [15] and although he addressed the issue of morality in almost everything he wrote, he did not consider himself a philosopher, much less a moral philosopher. Thus, to fully understand Buber's views on revelation, one would need to study the author's theological writings.

Thereafter, criticism of this notion as it appears in the ethical context would be much better informed.[16]

It is difficult to isolate the criticisms of Buber which focus on his ethics and specifically on that area of ethics which deals with the self and the Other. At first glance it would seem as if this area is entirely what morality is all about, but such is not the case. Therefore, to review extensively the commentary on this aspect of Buber's work would take us far afield, without providing significant insights into the ontology of the author. The reader who wishes to pursue the topic of ethics in the writings of Buber is referred to Maurice Friedman's excellent essay in *The Philosophy of Martin Buber*,[17] as well as to the numerous books and articles which have been published in this country and abroad.

Jean Wahl has written[18] that in some major aspects of their respective ontologies, Buber and Heidegger appear to be in agreement, especially if the later writings of Heidegger are examined. Buber's criticisms of Heidegger as well as his comments on Kierkegaard, according to Wahl, seem to ignore these authors' later writings which contradict, as it were, their earlier pronouncements. For example, the Danish philosopher's phrase, "If I had had faith, I would have remained with Regina" prompted Buber to remark that no one can refute Kierkegaard more forcefully than Kierkegaard himself. Buber was aware, then, that Kierkegaard did not advocate the avoidance of human contact in order to reach God. Similarly with regard to Heidegger, Wahl feels that Buber interprets the *Mitsein* rather narrowly . . .

> The Heideggerian *Selbst* open to the world has nothing of the isolated self of classical philosophies, and one cannot claim that it is a closed system (as Buber does in *The Knowledge of Man*). Buber would grant this, not doubt, since he writes that Heidegger does not see the highest stage of the self as an isolation but as consent through resolute

decision to the Mitsein, along with others; and he sees perfectly that the Heideggerian man does not sever himself from the world, but arrives by a resolute decision at a Dasein which is with the world.[19]

Wahl finds further evidence of the affinity between Buber and Heidegger, with minor exceptions, in their points of view on being-for-death and, most importantly, on their awe for the divine form. Granted that in the early writings of Heidegger, man was unable to communicate with the absolute. Still, Wahl notes, it would be incorrect to say that Heidegger's only concern, at that time, was with the relationship of Dasein to its own being. Nor is it accurate to place Heidegger in complete opposition to St. Augustine, Pascal and Kierkegaard, as Buber has done, according to Wahl, for Heidegger, in his more recent writings, also "seeks a divine aspect of being with which to converse and towards which he holds out his hands."[20] Moreover, Wahl claims, Heidegger asserts that "human life has its absolute meaning in the fact that it transcends its own character; yes, man can enter into relationship with other beings who are no less real to him than himself." To the extent that Wahl limits himself to the later Heidegger, it is indisputable that there is some affinity between the views of the two authors. Nevertheless, there is a sharp difference of emphasis and a divergent view on the appearance of the self (or Dasein) in the world. For Buber, the self comes-to-be as he enters into relation; for Heidegger, he is "thrown" into the world.

In view of the present study, it is notable that very little is said in Wahl's essay on "Buber and the Philosophers of Existence" about the similarities and differences between Buber and Sartre. To be sure, reference is made to the former's statement regarding a person's discovering values, not inventing them, and a curious allusion to Sartre's theory of communication suggests that "we have in Being and Nothingness but a portion of what it should be in its totality; to be exact, the portion consecrated to bad faith and to man as an object."[21] But other than these superficial remarks, Wahl contents himself with quoting or paraphrasing the few comments which Buber has made about some of Sartre's statements. One can only surmise that Wahl, in his eagerness to touch upon every "existentialist" writer of his day, judged it appropriate to mention a good number of them but to examine only one or two notions of each in relation to the philosophy of Buber.

In contrast to Wahl's sweeping comparison between Buber and such writers as Kierkegaard, Heidegger, Sartre, Jaspers, Marcel, Barth and several others, Paul E. Pfuetze approached his topic with depth and precision. Writing on Buber and Pragmatism,[22] and recognizing that if he tried to include all the major American pragmatists in his essay he would be forced to do so superficially, Pfuetze chose to focus on one writer only, George Herbert Mead. The reason for choosing this particular writer is obvious. There is an uncanny similarity between numerous ideas of Mead and Buber, and yet each writer's treatment of these ideas is idiosyncratic. It would take us beyond the scope of this study to examine at length the many parallels between the two philosophies. Perhaps an illustration or two will suffice.

Mead wrote that three conditions must be met for the self to exist: (1) a mechanism for self-stimulation, e.g., language, (2) life in cooperative and reciprocal relations with others, and (3) the ability to "get over into the experience of the other, to experience 'from the other side.'"[23] Not only does the third condition correspond exactly to Buber's "experiencing the other," (even the language sounds strangely similar) the second and first conditions are fully in agreement with Buber's thought. Pfuetze lists the following points of contact between Buber's existentialism and Mead's pragmatism:

> its anti-intellectualism, its stress on freedom; its functional active theory of

knowledge and meaning; its stress upon the act or deed; its *accent on social or interpersonal relations*; its emphasis upon *the reality and integrity of the* "other"; its taking of time and telic process seriously; its insistence upon the unity of theory and practice; the element of faith, venture, and immediate experience; its philosophy of speech; and most notably its social philosophy, with its central concept of what I have called the "social self," which sees the self as a *self-other*, I-Thou system, rather than as a mind.[24]

A closer examination of the two authors reveals, as can be expected, that they hold differing points of view on many issues. For example, Mead worked within a framework of secular behaviorism and was hostile to anything connected with the mystical, the transcendental. Buber felt comfortable expressing himself in the language of faith and revelation. In addition, whereas Buber conceived of man in a three-fold relation, to man, nature and God, Mead limited man's involvement to the dimension of human society only. Mead equated the ethical with the social. Buber believed that the eternal values are revealed by God in his relationship with man. Pfuetze is indeed perceptive in his analysis of the areas of where the two thinkers diverge as well as those in which their opinion is sympathetic. He is able to see these areas clearly because he fully understands the philosophers that he is comparing.

Given the number of essays which have been published to date on Buber's work, not to mention the books, articles, dissertations, etc., which surface every year and which seem to have increased in number since 1978 when the world celebrated the one hundredth year since Buber's birth, a section devoted to commentary on his philosophy must necessarily remain incomplete. Few critics will disagree that Buber's thought is not expressed in a tight, systematic manner. There is an internal cohesion, an impressive consistency in his views of dialogue, religion, ethics and anthropology, but as noted earlier, one must glean from all his writings the essential elements. Critics who focus on one aspect of his work, say, his view of revelation, or his interpretation of Hasidism in a manner which brings it in consonance with his own philosophy but risks distorting the actual Hasidic teaching,[25] may add to the understanding of the particular issue. It is doubtful that from such piecemeal assessments a significant critique of the author's complete philosophy can be made. Rather, the critics who address the starting points, e.g., that the essence of man is to be found in his relations or that the self comes into the world as the I utters Thou (or It), that is, the themes which recur in all of Buber's work, these critics point to alternative ways in which the same problems can be resolved. Those who explicate Buber render a great service to readers who need help in understanding him. But the critics who provide divergent viewpoints, their own or those of other philosophers, contribute generally to a better grasp of the subject, and consequently the reader can better appreciate the value or disvalue of the original argument.

Footnotes

1. See William A. Sadler, *Existence and Love* (New York: Charles Scribner's Sons, 1969), p. 104.

2. These two passages are quoted by Rotenstreich in "Buber's Dialogical Thought," in *PMB*, p. 127.

3. Martin Buber, "Beginning with Oneself," in *Hasidism and Modern Man* (New York: Harper & Row, 1966), pp. 154f.

4. Ibid., p. 156.

5. E.g., Sadler, *Existence and Love*, and Wheelwright, "Buber's Philosophical Anthropology," in *PMB*, p. 103.

6. Rotenstreich, "Buber's Dialogical Thought," in *PMB*, p. 97.

7. Charles Hartshorne, "Martin Buber's Metaphysics," in *PMB*, p. 53.

8. Ibid.

9. Ibid., p. 54.

10. Ibid.

11. Buber, *Eclipse of God*, pp. 118-19.

12. Marvin Fox, "Problems in Buber's Moral Philosophy," *PMB*, p. 156.

13. Buber, "Reply to my Critics," *PMB*, pp. 699-700.

14. He does say that the relation between divine address and human response is an antinomy which our understanding cannot resolve--*I and Thou*, p. 95.

15. Buber, *Eclipse of God*, p. 95.

16. Emil L. Fackenheim, in his essay, "Buber's Concept of Revelation," *PMB*, p. 273, does exactly that with reference to revelation, and the results are illuminating indeed.

17. Maurice Friedman, "The Bases of Buber's Ethics," in *PMB* p. 171.

18. Jean Wahl, "Buber and the Philosophies of Existence," in *PMB*, p. 475.

19. Ibid., p. 497.

20. Ibid., p. 498.

21. Ibid., p. 502.

22. Paul E. Pfuetze, "Martin Buber and American Pragmatism," in *PMB*, p. 511.

23. Ibid., p. 522.

24. Ibid., p. 527 (emphasis mine).

25. It was reported, by eye-witnesses of my acquaintance, that upon his death in Jerusalem, members of one or more Hasidic sects lit a bonfire in front of Buber's home and in it they tossed the author's books about Hasidism.

CHAPTER VI

CONCLUSION

If a philosopher's ontology were exclusively influenced by his religious beliefs, then Buber's ontology and Sartre's ontology would be _toto coelo_ different, and even opposite. After all, Buber's entire work is permeated by a deep-rooted commitment, intellectual as well as existential, to Hebraic teachings, Talmudic studies, Hasidic wisdom, and Judeo-Christian theology, whereas Sartre's philosophy was significantly less influenced by religious ideas. Still, in declaring that man must abandon any belief in God in order to more fully comprehend the freedom that is man's, Sartre was rejecting, for reasons about which one can only speculate, the religious notions inculcated into him as a youth.

In a way, Buber's ontology and Sartre's ontology are very different from one another. Yet, they meet at crucial points, and in particular in the recognition that "the Other" is a basic _ontological_ (not only an existential) problem. How is this possible?

One reason is the "existential horizon" in which both authors developed their respective ontologies. Another is that both Buber's "theism" and Sartre's "atheism" are forms of religious belief. Atheism is not religious indifference; it is a religious denial of positive religious beliefs.

Hence Buber and Sartre express often similar views as regards the cencept of the Other. For example, both writers emphasize that the Other is _wholly_ other. He is not a figment of one's imagination, not the product of introspection, not discoverable by analogy. He is so much an Other, for Sartre, that he poses a threat to me. He is so real to Buber, that only he can enable me to be wholly "I." Both writers make a certain metaphysical assumption, although both shy away from offering metaphysical statements. That is, that the self is a unity, and that the Other is equally a unity. There is no possible manner in which two people can be "as one." It is important in the ontologies of both authors that every human being be viewed as an individual creature.

Sartre, the declared existentialist, and Buber, who shunned all "isms," shared the belief that the Other needs me, and I him, in order to be made more fully aware of who and what he is and I am. Both authors embrace political ideologies which set a priority on the group, the community, the collective effort to better society's lot. Buber and Sartre excelled at describing inauthentic behavior. The former was content to do so in his essays,[1] but Sartre, having provided a phenomenological description of bad faith in *Being and Nothingness*, created, in addition, some unforgettable fictional characters[2] whose inauthentic modes of life are a vivid illustration of self-deception.

These similar views notwithstanding, the two writers differ on some fundamental issues. For example, a significant contrast lies in the fact that Buber considers the Other as important as the self (since I can rise to full self-being only in proportion to the self-being of the other, addressed as Thou; he and I share equally in existence), whereas for Sartre, as we have seen, the Other stands in my way, and I in his. We may succeed in alternating moments of capturing each other's freedom, but at no time can we expect to be together, both free, and not feel threatened. It is from this major difference that many other conflicts arise. Understandably, concrete relations with the Other are explained quite differently by the two writers.

Sartre's ontology, as noted, indicates an outlook on life that can be described as cynical, egoistical, individualistic, but nevertheless one in which great value is placed on commitment, not only to one's freedom but also to that of all humanity. Buber's ontology also points to interpersonal values. For both, the group, the community, etc., is as important as the person. But in contradistinction to Sartre's, Buber's ontology provides a framework within which the individual also is seen in harmony with his fellow men. Not afraid of what harm may be done, Buber's individual is free to go out toward the Other openly, and in so doing he affects both himself and the Other, in the core of their being and in their relationship. For Sartre, man is a "useless passion." For Buber, man has "made the earth into a garden."[3]

Perhaps the clearest area in which the divergence between Buber and Sartre can be viewed is that of sexuality. We have seen that Sartre elaborated extensively on his views regarding "concrete relations with the other," in the section of **Being and Nothingness** in which he examines minutely the notions of love, masochism, desire, hate, and sadism.[4] Buber, in his essay, "**Dialogue**," and in **Good and Evil**, agrees with Sartre on several important points: that sex in human beings is ontologically different from sex in other creatures, that it can never be analyzed in isolation from the interpersonal situation, that in sexual relations a person transcends himself or herself in relation to the Other, and that in such relations there is always an element of facticity. For buber, sex is a passion which, like all passions, must be given rational, decisive direction, otherwise, left undirected, it can become evil.

As Friedman explains,

What counts here is not the expression, repression or sublimation of sexual desire but the response with one's whole being that diverts our powerful desires from the casual to the essential. We are not to turn away from the things that attract our hearts but to get in touch with them by making our relationship to them essential and real.[5]

Radically different from Sartre's incarnation of the Other's freedom in the sexual act, Buber's account stresses the importance of "experienceing the real" in the other. He writes:

> A man caresses a woman who lets herself be caressed. Then let us assume that he feels the contact from two sides—with the palm of his hand still, and also with the woman's skin. The twofold nature of this gesture, as one that takes place between two persons, thrills through the depth of enjoyment in his heart and stirs it. (BMM 96)

In sex, as in other encounters between human beings, the Other, in Sartre's work, is viewed as an antogonist. In Buber's ontology the Other is a potential source of confirmation, the bridge to the Eternal Thou, the being without whom our existence, our thought, indeed the world, would be without meaning. Both writers recognize the importance of the Other for the coming-to-be of the self into the world. In Sartre's system man should be forewarned that he cannot help but come-to-be as "master" or "slave." He must disarm or be disarmed, capture the Other's freedom or allow the Other to capture his. In sex he must be sadistic or masochistic, indifferent or full of hate. There is no ontological basis in Sartre's work for genuine interpersonal love. In Buber's writings the self comes-to-be in genuine relation, or else he orients himself through I-It relations until such time as he succeeds in entering into dialogue. The possibility is always there—man needs but to avail himself of it.

Another area in which the divergence between the two writers' viewpoints is marked is the ethics which is or can be derived from their ontology. It has been argued by Warnock[6] and Bernstein,[7] among others,[8] that Sartre's ontology precludes an ethics. For this reason, his critics say, Sartre has not been able to keep his promise, made on the last page of *Being and Nothingness*, to devote a future work to the examination of ethics. Indeed, Sartre never wrote such a work, but his other writings provide ample material from which an ethical viewpoint can be glimpsed.

Warnock notes that there are ethical allusions in Sartre's later work, notably *CRD*, but she claims that the ethical writing was made possible only after Sartre had abandoned his earlier position. It was *after* his "radical conversion" from existentialism to Marxism, she points out, that Sartre began to consider the ethical dimension. Bernstein finds that the phenomenological description of man as human consciousness attempting to become God (i.e., striving in vain to transcend its contingency by becoming its own foundation; or, in other words, to be *causa sui*) commits man to inevitable bad faith. And bad faith being the inevitable human condition, Bernstein claims, it is meaningless to talk about morality in the Sartrean system.

Anderson's book has rebutted convincingly the notion that an ethics is incompatible with the Sartrean ontology.[9] Indeed, moral arguments in impressive numbers are shown to be expressed or implied in the pages of *Being and Nothingness*. An ethics can be constructed with Sartre's raw material; and for want of a more explicit formulation it is this ethics which can be compared to Buber's moral philosophy. It should be remembered that Buber's system is not so complete as to encompass a well disciplined, carefully written ethics, either. In this area, as in all his writings, Buber merely proposed to "point the way," to lead his reader to the window and show him what lies outside.

The comparison between Sartre's and Buber's ethics is still more difficult to make because of the divergence in *emphasis* by each writer. Sartre is concerned with the self-realization of the individual.

He takes great pains to explain the subtleness of bad faith, the myriad tricks the for-itself attempts in order to abrogate responsibility, to escape the burden that is its freedom and, in vain, to try to become in-itself. Buber, on the other hand, emphasizes the Other as a partner whose confirmation is a prerequisite to the healthy being of the self. There is no difference of opinion on the view that man is free, that his freedom entails a moral responsibility, that his actions affect the existence of other human beings. The difference lies in Sartre's heavy emphasis on the burden that is man's freedom vis-a-vis Buber's insistent stress on the effect of the attitude of the self toward the Other. One is brought back, after a careful examination of the two moral philosophies, to the essential difference which marks the two ontologies. In the Sartrean system the Other is viewed as an antagonist--and rules of conduct toward this foe can be drawn up to provide fairness in the conflict which is inevitable. There can be "counsels of prudence" drawn up too. In the Buberian system the Other is the person whose assistance in becoming a self is indispensable, and in this system, too, allowance is made for rules of conduct which ensure the well-being of both participants.

Are values invented, or discovered? Is God in eclipse, or is God dead? Is the ideal societal organization the group-in-fusion which becomes institutionalized, or is it the community of a kibbutz which provides maximum opportunities for dialogical relationships? These are questions which touch upon ethics only tangentially. They are more profitably examined within the context of sociology, theology and ontology.

Since both authors address questions of psychotherapy (Sartre wrote a section on "Existential Psychoanalysis" in *Being and Nothingsness*. Buber wrote "Guilt and Guilt Feelings" in *The Knowledge of Man*, "Healing Through Meeting" in *Pointing the Way*, and numerous essays which appeared in various journals of psychiatry), one is tempted to compare and contrast their views on this subject which is so closely related to their conception of man. Unfortunately, Sartre's comments are limited to a critique of a particular school of psychology, namely, that which strips a person of his individuality and concentrates instead on empirical symptomology which is shared by other individuals with the same diagnosis. Buber could not agree more with Sartre on this point. It is the whole person who must be treated. Sartre alludes to Flaubert again and again as some one whom psychologists have objectified, treated as in-itself, as it were, and not allowed for the share the novelist had in shaping his own character. Buber is more thorough in the examination of questions regarding pathology, therapy, and psychology. A comparison between the two writers is almost impossible on this account, since there is nothing available from Sartre which could be held up in contrast to Buber's views.

Mention should be made for the sake of completeness that Buber influenced a number of contemporary psychotherapists--among them Hans Trüb, Viktor van Weizsäker, Ludwig Binswanger, Arie Sborowitz, Eric Fromm, Carl R. Rogers, and, by now, entire schools of therapists who were inspired by these men. Buber's notions in this area were the logical extension of his anthropology. The therapist must confirm the patient as someone of value who needs to be helped in becoming capable of conducting his life in a rewarding manner. Whatever meaning life may have, it must be discovered and created by the individual whose existence is in question. Drugs can do no more than postpone the moment when, with all the resources of clear thinking and awareness available to the patient, he must succeed in assuming responsibility for himself. Manipulation, the attempt to instill a sense of security and confidence, hints on how to orient oneself through the difficulties of life, reassurance that everybody else (or many other people) feel(s) depressed, frustrated, afraid of pain, of being abandoned, of death, do little more for the patient than provide some false and tenuous relief from the anxiety which besets him. From this principle, Rogers developed the method of "client-centered therapy"[10] in which the psychiatrist strives to understand, feel and perceive the world as the client does, through the client's own eyes, as it were. Buber would say that the therapist must experience the real, he must be truly present, he must stand his ground but at the same time allow the client to stand his own, no matter how shaky.

From an adequate understanding of Sartre's philosophy, we can assume that he would not have concurred with Buber's views on the subject of psychotherapy. As with ethics, there is an important divergence on the starting point: what is man? For Buber, the Other can help or be helped in restoring mental health. Sartre, in holding that the Other is a rival, would have a difficult time working out a program through which a client could be helped. Indeed, the Other as the person who "_looks at me_," could be considered by the patient as someone who can help most of all by disappearing and thereby allowing the patient to be. That may be the reason for Sartre's silence on this issue in a chapter which purports to take up the topic of Existentialist Psychoanalysis.

It is significant that at the Eighth Congress of French Language Philosophical Societies,[11] the seventy-six articles submitted (and subsequently published[12] were grouped into three main symposia. As can be expected, the topics varied widely, and the range of interests reflected in the articles points to the diversity of specialties among the participants. Nevertheless, one of the symposia dealt with the theme of _Dialogue_. The other two focused on (1) _Psychopathology_ and (2) relationships between adults and youth. These are areas of study in which Buber specialized. Sartre, as it were, was not represented.

One commentator, Walter B. Goldstein, admittedly not unbiased, has characterized and drawn the consequences of Buber's dialogical philosophy in contrast to Existentialism (by which he means Sartrean Existentialism) in the form of a diagram:[13]

EXISTENTIALISM	DIALOGICAL PHILOSOPHY
Starting Point:	
Kierkegaard	Kierkegaard
Retains Kierkegaard's form	Changes Kierkegaard's form
Turns away from the environment	Turns toward the environment
Changes the content of Kierkegaard	Retains the content of Kierkegaard
Denies God	Assents to the God of Kierkegaard and Buber
Result:	
The self is isolated	Fundamentally the self is always related
Fundamental Issue:	
Existence precedes essence	Also valid in Dialogical Philosophy
Existence means realization	Also valid in Dialogical Philosophy
Realizations means activity, action	Also valid in Dialogical Philosophy
However: the isolated self can only realize itself through action.	The self realizes itself through its action, for the Thou, i.e., the Eternal Thou

Denial of God means denial of His revelation	God reveals Himself anew in every moment
Existentialists are the widowers of a dead God	The bearers of revelation are the ambassadors of the living God
The man of today is the man of crisis	For Buber also, he is "homeless"
This man has no objective standard anymore	Also true in Dialogical Philosophy
Therefore, he staggers about in a world of materiality,	Strides confidently along within nature,
which is not connected causally either with itself or with the self	which is definitely connected with itself and exists also as a Thou for the self
The self of crisis exists only in the relative	The self exists also in the world of turmoil
and is not connected to the absolute	and is connected to the Eternal Thou through all the relationships with persons addressed as Thou
[but] has, instead of the objective standard, only reference to itself	[but] has, instead of the objective standard, the reference to Thou and to the Eternal Thou

Result:

Solipsism	Altruism
Narcissism	Love of one's neighbor
Egomania	Helpfulness

Despair	Trust
Shipwreck	The new home of the world
A negative philosophy which breaks with the past	A positive philosophy which is founded on the past
and points to no path into the future	and unlocks the future

If one overlooks the hyperbolic expression and those claims which seem to be more emotional than reasoned (e.g., Buber=Altruism, Sartre=Egoism), one finds, nevertheless, that several notions which are opposed, as representing one or another of the philosophies, are valid illustrations of their respective points of view.

There appears to be a decrease in the popularity of so-called existentialist themes, such as man's freedom, the absurd, subjectivity, authenticity, the preference of solitude (as exemplified, for example, by Rousseau's *Les Rêveries d'un promeneur solitaire*, [14] or Montaigne's "De la solitude")[15] to losing oneself in a crowd. Overcoming the obstacles posed by an Other does not hold the challenge it once did. We have entered into a period in which good interpersonal relations are the life's ambition of many persons. To enter into genuine dialogical relationships has become more important than the ability to rely on one's own resources, to be "the master of one's fate." The "We" of which some far-seeing philosophers spoke in the past has become central in discussions about persons. In Pedagogy the "Affective Domain" refers to a hitherto neglected area of education. Accordingly, one of the chief objectives now is the development of skills which enable the individual to interact with the group in a manner that is rewarding to him as well as to the others. Psychotherapists and writers of "how to ____" books have been stressing the inner need for people to be assertive, responsive, knowledgeable about relationships.[16] Celibacy of priests is being questioned by numerous theologians within the Catholic

Church. These trends could be interpreted to reflect the influence of Buber, and from that one might be tempted to infer that Buber's ontology gives a clearer account than Sartre's. Such an inference, however, would not be justified by the detailed comparison which the present study has attempted.

Sartre and Buber have contributed more than any other writers to the understanding of the self and the Other. They approached the concept from divergent backgrounds, focused on divers aspects of it which each writer considered more important, and agreed essentially on perhaps the most basic insight to be derived from their researches, namely, that the awareness of self develops simultaneously with the consciousness of the Other. The fact that philosophers today prefer to address issues which <u>Buber</u> suggested does not preclude the possibility that <u>Sartre's</u> favorite themes may enjoy a renewal of interest in the future. Besides, popularity is only uncertainly correlated with intrinsic value.

Footnotes

1. Cf. the account of *being* and *seeming*, in "Elements of the Interhuman," *KM*, p. 77.

2. Cf. the senator in *la P-Respecteuse*, and the fascinating anti-heroes in *Les Chemins de la Liberté*.

3. Autobiographical Fragments, *PMB*, p. 38.

4. See above, pp. 127-28.

5. Maurice Friedman, "Sex in Sartre and Buber," *Review of Existential Psychology and Psychiatry*, III (1963): 119.

6. Warnock, *Existentialist Ethics*, pp. 45-50.

7. Richard Bernstein, *Praxis and Action* (Phila.: University of Pennsylvania Press, 1971), p. 149.

8. Among the numerous other writers who have expressed this view are Desan, Grene, Hartmann, Collins, and Friedman.

9. Thomas C. Anderson, *The Foundation and Structure of Sartrean Ethics* (Lawrence: Regent Press of Kansas, 1979).

10. Carl R. Rogers, *Client-Centered Therapy, Its Current Practice, Implications and Theory* (Boston: Houghton Mifflin Co., 1951).

11. Cf. p. 10 above.

12. Jankelevitch and Berger, editors, *L'Homme et son prochain*, contains the seventy-six articles. *La Présence d'autrui* contains special communications related to the Eigth Congress (Paris: Presses Universitaires, 1957).

13. Walter B. Goldstein, *Jean-Paul Sartre und Martin Buber: Eine vergleichende Betrachtung von Existentialismus und Dialogik*, (Jerusalem: Rubin Mass Verlag, 1965), pp. 38-40. (Emphasis mine).

14. Jean-Jacques Rousseau, *Les Rêveries d'un promeneur solitaire* (Paris: Garnier-Flammarion, 1964).

15. Michel de Montaigne, "De la Solitude," (Chap. XXIX), *Essais*, (Paris: Hachette, 1960).

16. A sampling of some titles illustrates this trend: S. B. Cotler and J. J. Guerra, *Assertion Training: A Humanistic Behavioral Guide to Self Dignity* (Champain, Ill.: Research Press, 1976). S. J. Smith, *When I Say No I Feel Guilty* (New York: Bantam Books, 1975). C. Schaeffer, *How to Influence Children: A Handbook of Practical Parenting Skills* (New York: Van Nostrand Reinhold Co., 1978). T. Harris, *I'm O.K., You're O.K.* (New York: Avon Books, 1976).

BIBLIOGRAPHY

I. **Primary Sources**

Works by Sartre

Sartre, Jean-Paul. *Les Chemins de la liberté*. Vol. I *L'Age de raison*, 1945; Vol. 2: *Le Sursis*, 1945; Vol. 3: *La Mort dans l'âme*, 1949. Paris: Gallimard.

. *Critique de la raison dialectique*. Paris: Gallimard, 1960. (English version: *Critique of Dialectical Reason*. Translated by Alan Sheridan-Smith; edited by Jonathan Ree. London: NLB; Atlantic Highlands; N.J.: Humanities Press, 1976.)

. *L'Etre et le néant*. Paris: Gallimard, 1943. (English version: *Being and Nothingness*. Translated by Hazel Barnes. New York: Philosophical Library, 1956.)

. "Existentialism." In *Existentialism from Dostoevsky to Sartre*, pp. 222-311. Edited by Walter Kaufmann. New York: World Publishing Co., 1965.

. *Huis Clos suivi de Les Mouches*. Paris: Gallimard, 1947.

. *La Nausée*. Paris: Gallimard, 1938.

. "Un Nouveau Mystique." In *Situations I*, pp. 143-88. Paris: Gallimard, 1947.

_____. "La Putain Respectueuse." In *Théâtre* (Les Mouches, Huis Clos, Morts san sépulture, La Putain Respectueuse). Paris: Gallimard. 1947.

Books and Articles About Sartre

Anderson, Thomas C. *The Foundation and Structure of Sartrean Ethics*. Lawrence: Regent Press of Kansas, 1979.

Barnes, Hazel. *An Existentialist Ethics*. New York: Alfred A. Knopf, 1967.

Bausola, Adrianno. *Liberta e relazioni interpersonali*: Introduzione alla lettura dell' "Essere e il nulla." Milano: Vita e Pensiero, Publicazioni dell' Universita Cattolica del Sacro Cuore, 1973.

Bernstein, Richard. *Praxis and Action*. Phila.: University of Pennsylvania Press, 1971.

Burkle, Howard R. "Sartre's 'Ideal' of Social Unity." In *Sartre*, pp. 315-36. Edited by Mary Warnock. Modern Studies in Philosophy. Anchor Books. Garden City, N.Y.: Doubleday & Co., 1971.

Catalano, Joseph. *A Commentary on Jean-Paul Sartre's "Being and Nothingness."* New York: Harper Torchbooks, Harper & Row, 1974.

Contat, Michel, and Rybalka, Michel. *Les Ecrits de Sartre*. Paris: Gallimard, 1970.

Desan, Wilfrid. *The Tragic Finale*. Cambridge: Harvard University Press, 1954.

Grene, Marjorie. "Sartre and Heidegger: The Free Resolve," and "Sartre and Heidegger: The Self and Other Selves." In *Dreadful Freedom*. 2nd ed. Chicago: Chicago University Press, 1960.

⸻⸻. *Sartre*. New York. Franklin Watts, 1973.

Hartmann, Klaus. *Sartre's Ontology: A Study of Being and Nothingness in the Light of Hegel's Logic*. Evanston: Northwestern University Press, 1966.

Jeanson, Francis. *Le Problème moral et la pensée de Sartre*. Paris: Editions du Seuil, 1965.

Kampits, Peter. *Sartre und die Frage nach dem anderen: eine sozialontologische Untersuchung*. Vienna: R. Oldenbourg Verlag, 1974.

Kern, Edith. "The Self and the Other: A Dilemma of Existential Fiction." *Comparative Literature Studies* 5, no. 3 (September 1968): 329-37.

Kline, George L. "Existentialist Rediscovery of Hegel and Marx." In *Sartre*, pp. 284-314. Edited by Mary Warnock. Modern Studies in Philosophy. Anchor Books. Garden City, N.Y.: Doubleday & Co., 1971.

Lapointe, François, and Lapointe, Claire. *Jean-Paul Sartre and his Critics: An International Bibliography* (1938-1975). Bowling Green, OH: Bowling Green University, Philosophy Documentation Center, 1975.

Lopez, Salgado, C. "El projimo en el existentialismo de Sartre." *Estudios de Teología y Filosofía*, 5 (1962):59-69.

Morris, Phyllis Sutton. *Sartre's Concept of a Person: An Analytic Approach*. Amherst: University of Massachusetts Press, 1976.

Natanson, Maurice. *A Critique of Jean-Paul Sartre's Ontology.* Lincoln, Neb.: University of Nebraska Studies, 1951.

Owens, Thomas. "Absolute aloneness as Man's Existential Structure: A Study of Sartrean Ontology." *New Scholasticism* 40 (1966):341-60.

Salvan, Jacques L. *To Be or Not to Be.* Detroit: Wayne State University Press, 1962.

Scanlon, John D. "Consciousness, the Streetcar, and the Ego: Pro Husserl, Contra Sartre." *Philosophical Forum* no. 2 (Spring 1971): 350.

Varet, Gilbert. *L'Ontologie de Sartre.* Paris: Presses Universitaires de France, 1948.

Warnock, Mary, ed. *Sartre.* Garden City, N.Y.: Doubleday & Co., 1971.

Works by Buber

Buber, Martin. *Between Man and Man.* Translated by Ronald Gregor Smith. New York: Macmillan Co., 1965. This volume contains the following essays: "Dialogue," 1929; "The Question to the Single One," 1936; "Education," 1926; "The Education of Character," 1939' "What is Man," 1938; "Afterword," 1964.

. *Eclipse of God.* Translated by Maurice Friedman. New York: Harper & Row, 1957. This volume contains the following essays: "Religion and Reality," "Religion and Philosophy," "The Love of God and the Idea of Deity," "Religion and Modern Thinking," "Religion and Ethics," "On the Suspension of the Ethical," "God and the Spirit of Man."

. *Good and Evil*. New York: Carles Scribner's Sons, 1952.

. *Hasidism and Modern Man*. New York: Harper & Row, 1958.

Buber, Martin. *I and Thou*. 2nd ed. Translated by Ronald Gregor Smith. New York: Charles Scribner's Sons, 1958.

. *Ich und Du*. Vol. I: Werke, Schriften zur Philosophie. Munich: Kosel, 1962.

. *The Knowledge of Man*. Edited and translated by Maurice Friedman. New York: Harper Torchbooks, 1960. This volume contains the following essays: "Distance and Relation," "Elements of the Interhuman," "What is Common to All," "The Word That is Spoken," "Guilt and Guilt Feelings," "Man and His Image Work," "Dialogue Between Martin Buber and Carl R. Rogers."

. *Paths In Utopia*. Boston: Beacon Press, 1958.

. *Pointing the Way*. Translated by Maurice Friedman. New York: Harper Torchbooks, Harper & Row, 1963.

. *Two Types of Faith*. Translated by Norman Goldhawk. New York: Harper Torchbooks, Harper & Row, 1961.

. "Ueber Jacob Boehme." *Wiener Rundschau* 5, no. 12 (June 15, 1901):251-53.

Books and Articles about Buber

Biser, Eugen. "Martin Buber." Philosophy Today 7, no. 2 (1963):108.

Fackenheim, Emil L. "Buber's Concept of Revelation." In The Philosophy of Martin Buber, pp. 273-96. Edited by Paul Arthur Schilpp and Maurice Friedman. The Library of Living Philosophers, Inc. La Salle, Ill: Open Court Press, 1967.

Fox, Marvin. "Problems in Buber's Moral Philosophy." In The Philosophy of Martin Buber, pp. 151-70. Edited by Paul Arthur Schilpp and Maurice Friedman. The Library of Living Philosophers. La Salle, Ill.: Open Court Press, 1967.

Friedman, Maurice S. Martin Buber: The Life of Dialogue. New York: Harper & Row, 1955.

⎯⎯⎯. "The Bases of Buber's Ethics." In The Philosophy of Martin Buber, pp. 171-200. Edited by Paul Arthur Schilpp and Maurice Friedman. The Library of Living Philosophers. La Salle, Ill.: Open Court Press, 1967.

Hartshorne, Charles. "Martin Buber's Metaphysics." In The Philosophy of Martin Buber, pp. 49-68. Edited by Paul Arthur Schilpp and Maurice Friedman. the Library of Living Philosophers. La Salle, Ill.: Open court Press, 1967.

Horwitz, Rivka. Buber's Way to I and Thou: An Historical Analysis of the First Publication of Martin Buber's Lectures "Religion als Gengenwart." Heidelberg: Verlag Lambert Schneider, 1978.

Moonan, Williard. *Martin Buber: An Annotated Bibliography of Scholarship in English*. New York: Garland Publishing, 1979.

Pfuetze, Paul E. "Martin Buber and American Pragmatism." In *The Philosophy of Martin Buber*, pp. 511-42. Edited by Paul Arthur Schilpp and Maurice Friedman. The Library of Living Philosophers. La Salle, Ill.: Open Court Press, 1967.

Pfuetze, Paul E. *Self, Society, Existence: Human nature and Dialogue in the Thought of George Herbert Mead and Martin Buber*. Westport, Conn.: Greenwood Press, 1973.

Rome, Sidney, and Rome, Beatrice, eds. *Philosophical Interrogations*. New York: Holt, Rinehart & Winston, 1964.

Rotensteich, Nathan. "The Right and the Limitations of Buber's Dialogical Thought." In *The Philosophy of Martin Buber*, pp. 97-132. Edited by Paul Arthur Schilpp and Maurice Friedman. The Library of Living Philosophers. La Salle, Ill.: Open Court Press, 1967.

Schaeder, Grete. *The Hebrew Humanism of Martin Buber*. Translated by Noah J. Jacobs. Detroit: Wayne State University Press, 1973.

Schilpp, Paul Arthur, and Friedman, Maurice, eds. *The Philosophy of Martin Buber*. The Library of Living Philosophers. La Salle, Ill.: Open Court Press, 1967.

Wahl, Jean. "Buber and the Philosophies of Existence." In *The Philosophy of Martin Buber*, pp. 475-510. Edited by Paul Arthur Schilpp and Maurice Friedman. The Library of Living Philosophers. La Salle, Ill.: Open Court Press, 1967.

Wood, Robert E. *Martin Buber's Ontology: An Analysis of I and Thou*. Evanston: Northwestern University Press, 1968.

Books and Articles About Sartre and Buber

Friedman, Maurice. "Sex in Sartre and Buber," *Review of Existential Psychology and Psychiatry* 3, no. 2 (1963): pp. 113-24.

Goldstein, Walter B. *Jean-Paul Sartre und Martin Buber: Eine vergleichende Betrachtung von Existentialismus und Dialogik*. Jerusalem: Rubin Mass Verlag, 1965.

Olafson, Fredrick A. *Principles and Persons: An Ethical Interpretation of Existentialism*. Baltimore: Johns Hopkins press, 1967.

Sadler, William A. *Existence and Love*. New York: Charles Scribner's Sons, 1969.

Warnock, Mary. *Existentialist Ethics*. New York: Macmillan & Co., and also St. Martin's Press, 1967.

II. Secondary Sources

Beauvoir, Simone de. *La Force des Choses*. Paris: Gallimard, 1963.

Chastaing, Maxime. *L'existence d'autrui*. Paris: Presses Universitaires de France, 1951.

Descartes, René. *Philosophical Works*. Translated by E. S. Haldane and G. R. T. Ross. New York: Dover Publications, 1955. [orig. published 1911.]

Driesch, Hans. *The Problem of Individuality*. London: Macmillan & Co., 1914.

Entralgo, Laín. *Teoría y Realidad del Otro*. 2 vols. Madrid: Revista de Occidente, 1961.

Hegel, Friedrich. *Philosophy of Mind. Part 3 of the Encyclopedia of the Philosophical Sciences*. Translated by William Wallace, together with the Zusätze in Boumann's text, translated by A. V. Miller. Clarendon: Oxford University Press, 1971.

Heidegger, Martin. *Being and Time*. [1927] Translated by John Macquarrie and Edward Robinson. New York: Harper & Row, 1962.

⸻. *An Introduction to Metaphysics*. Translated by Ralph Manheim. Garden City, N.Y.: Doubleday & Co., 1961.

⸻. *Vom Wesen Des Grundes*. Frankfurt Am Main: Klostermann, 1955.

Hodges, H.A. *The Philosophy of William Dilthey*. London: Routledge & Kegan Paul, 1952.

Husserl, Edmund. *Cartesian Meditations*. Translated by Dorian Cairns. The Hague: Martinus Nijhoff, 1970.

———. "The Crises of European Humanity and Philosophy." In *The Search for Being*. Translated and edited by Jean Wilde and William Kimmel. New York: Noonday, 1962.

Jankelevitch, Vladimir, and Berger, Gaston, eds. *L'Homme et son prochain*. Paris: Presses Universitaires, 1957.

———. *La Présence d'autrui*. Paris: Presses Universitaires, 1957.

Kainz, Howard P. *Hegel's Phenomenology, Part I: Analysis and Commentary*. Alabama: University of Alabama Press, 1976.

Kant, Immanuel. *Critique of Pure Reason*. Translated by Norman Kemp Smith. New York: St. Martin's Press, 1965.

———. *Groundwork of the Metaphysic of Morals*. Translated by H. J. Paton. New York: Harper Torchbooks, Harper & Row, 1968.

Kant, Immanuel. *Religion Within the Limits of Reason Alone*. Translated by Theodore M. Greene and Hoyt H. Hudson. New York: Harper Torchbooks, Harper & Row, 1960.

Katz, Jerrold J. *The Underlying Reality of Language and its Philosophical Import*. New York: Harper Torchbooks, Harper & Row, 1971.

Makkreel, Rudolf A. *Dilthey*. Princeton: Princeton University Press, 1975.

Merleau-Ponty, Maurice. *Phénoménologie de la perception*. Paris: Editions Gallimard, 1945.

Mounier, Emmanuel. *Existential Philosophies*. Translated by Eric Blow. New York: Macmillan Publishing Co., 1949.

Ortega y Gasset, José. *Concord and Liberty*. Translated by Helene Weyl. New York: W. W. Norton & Co., 1946.

Ortega y Gasset, José. *Man and People*. Translated by Willard R. Trask. New York: W. W. Norton & Co., 1957.

Paton, H. J. *The Categorical Imperative: A Study in Kant's Moral Philosophy*. New York: Harper Torchbooks, Harper & Row, 1967.

Ryle, Gilbert. *The Concept of Mind*. New York: Barnes & Noble, 1949.

Scheler, Max. *Der Formalismus in der Ethik und die materiale Wertethik*. Bern: Francke Verlag, 1954.

_____. *Man's Place in Nature*. Translated by Hans Meyerhoff. Boston: Beacon Press, 1961.

Scheler, Max. *The Nature of Sympathy*. Translated by Peter Heath. London: Routledge & Kegan Paul, 1970.

Thévanaz, Pierre. "What is Phenomenology?" In *What is Phenomenology? and Other Essays*, pp. 37-92. Edited by James M. Edie. Chicago: Quadrangle Books, 1962.

Wartofsky, Marx W. *Feuerbach*. Cambridge: Cambridge University Press, 1977.

Wheelwright, Phillip. "Buber's Philosophical Anthropology." In *The Philosophy of Martin Buber*, p. 82. Edited by Paul Arthur Schilpp and Maurice Friedman. The Library of Living Philosophers. La Salle, Ill.: Open Court Press, 1967.

Whitehead, Alfred North. *Symbolism: Its Meaning and Effect*. [1927] New York: Capricorn Books, G. P. Putnam's Sons, 1959.

III. Other Books and Articles Consulted or Mentioned in the Text

Cotler, S. B., and Guerra, J. J. *Assertion Training: A Humanistic Behavioral Guide to Self Dignity.* Champain, Ill.: Research Press, 1976.

Eliot, T. S. "The Love song of J. Alfred Prufrock." In *The Complete Poems and Plays 1909-1950*, pp. 3-7 New York: Harcourt Brace & World, 1952.

Harris, T. *I'm O.K., You're O.K.* New York: Avon Books, 1976.

Laing, Ronald D. *The Divided Self: An Existential Study in Sanity and Madness.* Baltimore: Penguin Books, 1965.

———. *Self and Others.* Baltimore: Penguin Books, 1971.

Montaigne, Michel. "De la solitude," (Ch. XXXIX) in *Essais*, pp. 130-37. Paris: Hachette, 1960.

Rogers, Carl R. *Client-Centered Therapy, Its Current Practice, Implications and Theory.* Boston: Houghton Mifflin Co., 1951.

Rousseau, Jean-Jacques. *Les Rêveries d'un promeneur solitaire.* Paris: Garnier-Flammarion, 1964.

Schaeffer, C. *How to Influence Children: A Handbook of Practical Parenting Skills.* New York: Van Nostrand Reinhold Co., 1978.

Smith, S. J. *When I Say No I feel Guilty.* New York: Bantam Books, 1975.